Kubrick's Cinema Odyssey

Michel Chion
Translated by Claudia Gorbman

 Publishing

First published in 2001 by the
British Film Institute
21 Stephen Street, London W1P 2LN

The British Film Institute promotes greater understanding of, and access to, film and
moving image culture in the UK.

Cover design: Mark Swan

Set in Italian Garamond by Fakenham Photosetting, Norfolk
Printed in England by Cromwell Press, Trowbridge, Wiltshire

British Library Cataloguing-in-Publication Data
A catalogue record for this book is available from the British Library
ISBN 0 85170 839 0 (pbk)
ISBN 0 85170 840 4 (hbk)

Contents

Preface

The year 2001 rekindles our interest in a legendary work and a cinematic masterpiece in its own right. Stanley Kubrick's *2001: A Space Odyssey* has been symbolic in several respects since its release in 1968. Not only did it set a new course for science-fiction cinema; it also merged the two streams of big, popular films and experiments in 'pure' cinema. In its sparse though essential dialogue, and in the way it foregrounds elements of film form itself – sound, light, movement, editing – *2001* is the father of all 'event movies', whose screenings have the aura of a religious rite. It draws on the sonic and visual experimentation of the early sound era as well as the 60s 'modernity' (Antonioni, Tati) from which it springs. In aspiring towards non-verbal, universal experience, it embodies the dream of absolute cinema.[1] Finally, it is among its director's most personal and daring films, a work that speaks to us in an extraordinarily strong way about the human condition.

Along with Jacques Tati's *Playtime* – another 'futuristic' montage released in the same year – *2001* represents one of the rare efforts made during the 60s by a great director to wrench widescreen and stereo sound away from the inevitable territory of the blockbuster-of-the-thousand-extras, and to offer instead a slow, allusive, contemplative work. It produced myths for our time (the bone metamorphosing into a spacecraft over a four-million-year ellipsis; the Strauss waltz accompanying images of outer space; the death of the computer) that have enriched movie history and world culture.

To be sure, *2001: A Space Odyssey* did not instantaneously spring forth as a classic. Its complex genesis illustrates the vicissitudes of the creative process, and the roles of chance, hesitation and determination.

2001 is a particularly fascinating film in that Kubrick exceeded the limits of his own perfectionism in making it, perhaps even more than in his other works. Intentional factors, when combined with the imponderables, doubts, technical problems and last-minute decisions and changes of mind, gave it dimensions it might otherwise not have had. Its creator thus could not measure the effects of many of his choices (especially his 'negative' choices, when he cut sequences already shot, or eliminated narrative elements), and it was a sign of his genius that he could allow his work to slip from his control, so that, rather than being merely the execution of a blueprint, it could attain the status of an impersonal masterwork.

A book of a thousand pages could not begin to do justice to all the dimensions of *2001*, one of the most widely discussed of all movies. I hope merely to open as many doors onto it as possible.

This book is multi-faceted, owing to my own desire to propose to readers a text on multiple levels and in complementary parts. The historical sections bring together and organise for the first time information and perspectives from many sources, including some that may be new to English-speaking readers. The more analytical and theoretical sections complement and extend the overall concerns of my critical writing begun in the book *The Voice in Cinema*.[2]

A final chapter is devoted to *Eyes Wide Shut*, a film that came out after I began writing. In my estimation, *Eyes Wide Shut* is both a codicil to Kubrick's oeuvre and an answer to *2001*.

My sincere thanks go to Michel Ciment, Bruno Follet and especially Michel Marie for their help in the evolution of this book.

M. C., 17 July 1999

Notes

1   We shall see how the notion of a non-verbal cinema can only be conceived dialectically.

2   *La Voix au cinéma* (Paris: Éditions de l'Étoile, 1982). English translation Claudia Gorbman (New York: Columbia University Press, 1999).

Chapter One
The Genesis of *2001*

Arthur C. Clarke's 'The Sentinel'

Shot in England where Kubrick lived, *2001* had had a long and complex gestation. Kubrick eventually removed an enormous amount of the screenplay's original narrative scaffolding (a documentary prologue about aliens, a voice-over commentary, Alex North's epic score), a scaffolding that at the outset was an integral part of the project, and without the support of which he doubtless could not have constructed this singular film.

It was also Kubrick's intention to bring special effects and models to an unprecedented level of perfection and to depict weightlessness more convincingly than ever – in other words, to create a world governed by new laws.

His previous film, *Dr Strangelove*, was a great popular success, and Kubrick was hailed by the New York Film Critics Circle as Best Director of 1964. At that time he was interested in the question of the existence of extraterrestrials, and began to think about collaborating with the English science-fiction writer Arthur C. Clarke, author of (among many other works) a 1948 short story entitled 'The Sentinel', which would provide a point of departure for *2001*.

In this brief piece, whose action is set in 1996, a geologist exploring the moon's surface discovers an object shaped like a pyramid. It has been there for a very long time and was clearly constructed by 'someone'. Its purpose is unknown (a building? a shrine?). But the geologist makes another surprising discovery: this object was preserved from meteorite attacks and cosmic dust by a sort of invisible hemispheric wall; stones thrown against it bounce off, proving that it is still being protected by active forces and is not the product of some defunct lunar civilisation. In a word, the object comes from elsewhere.

It takes twenty years of work to break through its invisible shield, whereupon closer examination indicates that a highly evolved technology from another solar system produced it. Whoever put it there, speculates the narrator, must have landed on the moon a very long time ago. They must have determined that the earth had the most suitable environment in the solar system for intelligent life, and then placed this monument on its satellite as an outpost sentinel, so that man would only see it if he attained a sufficiently high degree of evolution to be able to leave the 'cradle' of his own planet – and (the other necessary condition) if he has not already destroyed his species with the atomic energy he has unleashed. Now that the sentinel has been discovered and its protective shield forced open, it has stopped emitting its signal. Maybe those who left it there will show themselves, unless they are too old and in decline. The only thing to do from here on, says the narrator, is to wait; but 'I do not think we will have to wait for long.'[1]

Even if the screenplay by Kubrick and Clarke would end up being far more complex, bearing only a distant relationship to this short story, it is interesting to see the germ of several elements that remained in the film. There is, of course, the idea of an object left on the moon for centuries; there is also the secret relationship between the object and mankind's mastery of the nuclear menace. We know that in the film the object did not end up in the form of a four-sided pyramid. In addition, instead of the idea of an invisible shield, the screenplay presents a monolith that has been deliberately buried; this substitution gives the object the equivalent of a protective shield, and similarly poses a challenge to humans, and suggests intention ('Show that you are strong and smart enough to find me'). In the film, the earsplitting signal heard by the humans who start to photograph the object further suggests that the object is being protected.

The notion of the earth as a cradle that man must eventually leave also finds an echo in the finished film – ending up in the form of a gigantic Star Child, a baby who for the first time seems to be born into space and goes without maternal protection. *The impossibility of escaping from the cradle* seems to me to be at the heart of Kubrick's work, and the feeling of fatality that emerges from it. Finally, the main thread running through the short story is the verb *to wait*, and clearly *2001*, with each of its different parts setting the stage for the next, is subtended by the idea of waiting, of Advent (to take an associated word in Christian tradition that prepares for Christmas).

'The Sentinel' was a 4000-word short story written in 1948 for a Christmas story contest sponsored by the BBC, which rejected it. Clarke's text was not published until 1951, as one of thirteen stories by various authors, in a short-lived magazine called *10 Story Fantasy*. It was the author who exhumed it for Kubrick.

Evolution of the Screenplay

When Kubrick met Clarke in 1964 in order to develop ideas for a film about extraterrestrials, it was not especially this particular story he had in mind; rather, his interest was in the author, who had a reputation for writing 'adult' science fiction. Clarke, informed by Kubrick's publicist Roger Caras of Kubrick's desire to work with him, sent Caras a telex: 'Frightfully interested in working with enfant terrible stop contact my agent stop what makes kubrick think I'm a recluse.'[2]

It is an interesting coincidence that each of the two artists became an expatriate. Just as Kubrick rarely left his home near London, so Clarke moved to Ceylon (now Sri Lanka) in 1956 in order to write – later boasting that his practice of working out of his home before anyone else was a precursor of electronic mail.

Born in 1917, Clarke served as president of astronautic societies[3] and, in addition to his novels, was the author of a large number of popular science books. He is an exemplar, in the very diverse field of classic Anglo-Saxon science fiction, of the tendency to base fictional speculations on actual current science. Other science-fiction authors, such as Van Vogt, Philip Jose Farmer and Theodore Sturgeon, belong in the tradition of Lovecraft or mythic, fantastic or heroic fiction – not to mention the Swiftian or Voltairean strain represented by Robert Sheckley – and bother little with astronomical or technical authenticity. Two themes that recur through Clarke's novels are contact with other civilisations, as in *Rendezvous with Rama*, and the question of the survival and regeneration of humanity, especially prominent in *Childhood's End*.

'The Sentinel' is one of several short stories that Clarke and Kubrick briefly considered combining, before they made the decision to use it by itself as their point of departure. In May 1964, a contract was signed 'for a film whose preparation was to last eighty-two weeks, until February 1967, the expected date of the Apollo programs'.[4]

Clarke's *The Lost Worlds of 2001* narrates in detail his version of this collaboration, and retraces the different forms the screenplay took as well as the many ideas that arose and evolved or fell by the wayside. First of all, they did not want to situate the film too far in the future, though they were eager not to have it become outmoded too soon either. They wanted to bring in the theme of machines, with a perfected robot; after a period as an ambulatory robot called Athena (referring to the protector of Odysseus in Homer), this 'character' became an invisible computer by the name of Hal.[5] In its early stages, the screenplay dealt more with Russian–American relations, depicting the two countries working together. The authors also thought of giving extraterrestrials a role in the birth of humanity (the idea of marking the progress of evolution by the move to carnivorous existence is imputed to Kubrick, which does not surprise me). Finally, there is the idea of a kind of evolutionary process whereby ever more perfect machines take over from mankind.

This last idea, which continued to fascinate Kubrick (one of his last projects, which was well progressed when he died, concerned artificial intelligence), takes an unexpected turn in the film. *2001* allows us to imagine that these hypothetical invisible aliens who have 'abducted' Bowman possess technology a thousand times superior to our own. However, as the film in its final state shows nothing specific or recognisable of the aliens' machines, we are also perfectly free to imagine the extraterrestrials as gods, and to read *2001* as an *anti*-technology film by drawing on old, mystical notions of power. In early versions of the screenplay, the neoclassical decor of Dave's 'bedroom' has been created by robots. But if Kubrick chose to leave this undetermined in the final script, it is not so that we should reread the film in the light of his original intentions. The earlier ideas interest me as stages in a genesis, and not as the unveiling of a hidden meaning.

We know that Kubrick abhorred the idea of directly writing *2001* in the conventional form of a movie screenplay, 'the most uncommunicative form of writing ever devised'.[6] So he decided to write a novel with Clarke that would serve as the basis for making the film.

During the preparation and writing phase, which took place in New York (Clarke rented suite 1008 at the Chelsea Hotel), Kubrick got together to discuss ideas with a variety of scholars and artists, including Carl Sagan (whose writings inspired Robert Zemeckis's film *Contact*).

Kubrick was so immersed in his project that sometimes he worried that real-life events might overtake his film and render it obsolete: for example, what if aliens were really discovered? What could his film possibly offer audiences then?

Late in 1964, a first version of the story (whose ending left the hero on the threshold of the Star Gate) was ready in novel form, permitting Kubrick to secure a contract with MGM and Cinerama. The film would be shot in 70mm Super Panavision (and part in 35mm) but would have the Cinerama label.[7] Cinerama was originally a system that used three cameras side by side and, although its technical definition changed in the early 60s, prints continued to be struck in the three-image format and shown in a number of theatres equipped for this gigantic projection. For wider distribution, Cinerama movies made during the 60s – including *How the West Was Won* (1962), which used the three-image system, and *2001*, in single-image format – were, after the first run, distributed in 35mm CinemaScope copies, with the corresponding loss in definition and the frame format changes that this entailed.

In 1965, a *New Yorker* article described the shooting of a film with a working title of *Journey Beyond the Stars* (the movie already made conscious reference to *2001*). Athena's name was now Hal, having undergone a period as Socrates. Work on the screenplay, however, was stalled by numerous second thoughts and changes of mind, and the plan to release the film, already delayed in an announcement by MGM president Robert O'Brien who set it for Christmas 1966 or spring 1967 at the latest, was delayed further still.

In an interview in the *New Yorker* during pre-production in 1965, Clarke announced that the film 'is set in the near future, at a time when the moon will have been colonized and space travel, at least around the planetary system, will have become commonplace'. Kubrick and Clarke characterised the film as an encounter with extraterrestrials: 'the Odyssey unfolds as our descendants attempt to make contact with some extraterrestrial explorers'.[8]

Clarke continued, 'There will be no women among those who make the trip, although there will be some on earth, some on the moon, and some working in space.'[9] As we know, not much of this remains in the film. The women we see in *2001* are flight attendants, receptionists or hostesses, or they stay on earth, embodying the stability and the permanence of the family (Floyd's daughter, Poole's mother). The film does, however, sketchily present Elena, a Russian scientist who works on the moon and tells Floyd about her husband back on earth who studies the depths of the Baltic, so 'I am afraid we don't get the chance to see each other these days.'

In the same 1966 interview, Clarke told Jeremy Bernstein, 'Science-fiction films have always meant monsters and sex, so we have tried to find another term for our film.'[10] Before *2001*, popular science fiction was intimately associated with sexuality, strange as that may seem to us today. Young starlets in skimpy clothing (Anne Francis in *Forbidden Planet* or Yvette Mimieux in *The Time Machine*), lascivious blondes, nymphets abducted by monsters or giving orders to robots, all figured prominently. Travel to new worlds could not be conceived without a beautiful creature like Raquel Welch in *Fantastic Voyage* (Richard Fleischer, 1966), a movie in which a miniaturised team explores the cosmos inside a human body (certain shots of the Star Gate trip in *2001* are also obviously conceived to suggest a voyage through the body).[11] *2001*'s stewardess in very decent garb who can walk upside down in zero gravity, adhering to the floor by means of Velcro-soled bootees, was Kubrick's chaste answer to an image that appeared on movie screens at almost the same time: Jane Fonda's weightless striptease in Roger Vadim's *Barbarella*, inspired by Jean-Claude Forest's French comic strip.

Kubrick affirmed that he was a great reader of science fiction, but also made clear his intention to make a film that would be true to the state of contemporary physics and astronomy, and expressed amazement at the public's ignorance of up-to-date scientific knowledge. In the official communiqué announcing the start of production on the film at the beginning of 1965, the director gave this description of the project:

> *Journey Beyond the Stars* is an epic story of adventure and exploration, encompassing the Earth, the planets of our Solar System, and a journey light-years away to another part of the Galaxy. It is a scientifically based yet

dramatic attempt to explore the infinite possibilities th
opens to mankind. The great biologist J. B. S. Haldan
not only stranger than we imagine; it is stranger than
you consider that in our Galaxy there are a hundred *b*
our Sun is a perfectly average specimen, and that present estimates put the
number of Galaxies in the visible Universe at a hundred *million*, Haldane's
statement seems rather conservative.[12]

This description is quite vague regarding the actual narrative events of the
project. Kubrick insisted on maintaining a veil of secrecy, for he wanted
the option of being able to change anything at any time – the film was never
based on a scenario that could be considered as set in stone. Everything
was left open until the last possible moment.

2001: Film and Novel

The comparison with the novel of the same name published upon the film's
release, with the single signature of Arthur C. Clarke but specifying that it
was 'Based on a screenplay by Stanley Kubrick and Arthur C. Clarke', obviously does not have the meaning it would normally have in the case of an
adaptation. On the contrary, the novel, dedicated 'to Stanley', rather clev-
erly adopts an opposite position to that of the film. Probably in order to
avoid being merely a written paraphrase of the film, it describes and
explains everything much more explicitly, leaving nothing to interpretation.
Yes, Clarke tells us, the monolith is a sort of device that causes the more
evolved apes to attain a stage of abstraction and superior intelligence without their ever knowing what hit them. Yes, the novel allows us to enter the
primitive mind of 'Moonwatcher', the chief of the ape tribe, so we can follow the progression of his questions and revelations. Yes, the hypotheses
that come to our minds regarding the nature of the monolith (tomb, monument, landmark) are formulated explicitly; the narrator deals with them,
sometimes even a character as well. The novel also tells us a little more
about the moon base (1600 men and 700 women are stationed there),
about the monolith (its proportions are 1:4:9, or the squares of 1, 2 and
3), and about why the monument emits the electromagnetic screech at the
very moment the men try to photograph it – it coincided with the light from

sun hitting it for the first time in four million years. It identifies the antenna, of whose imminent failure Hal warns the astronauts, as their sole link, 'small but vital', with the earth – a fact not stated in the film. And in the novel, Bowman feels grief, if only for a moment, when Poole dies. Yes, the bedroom suite where Dave lands is an artefact of earth, fabricated by the aliens based on television images they have seen. And so on.

Furthermore, in Chapter 27, we enter into the tormented 'consciousness' of Hal the computer, a consciousness that the novelist artificially bestows on him (the film-maker refrains from doing so). Clarke gives precise explanations for his behaviour: 'He had been brooding over the secret he could not share with Poole and Bowman. He had been living a lie ...'

Which is why he then acts as he does. But we must not see Kubrick's work in the light of the book and some of the explanations it furnishes, because doing so would rob the film of the many ambiguities that give it its richness. Let us say, once and for all, the film and the book are two different and autonomous works.

In the novel Clarke returned to an idea that the film had to abandon for purely technical reasons. The novel established the Star Gate on a moon of Saturn, Japetus. Jupiter had actually been the first idea for the screenplay, abandoned in favour of Saturn, then ultimately readopted.

But the most significant difference in dramatic terms is that in the novel, Dave does not lose all communication with the earth after disconnecting Hal. Instead, he is contacted by the base, by Floyd, who explains to him what happened with Hal 9000. Floyd remains in contact with Dave right up to the point when the hero enters another world, that of the 'explorers'; Dave leaves his last sentence to our planet in the form of an exclamation: 'Oh my God! *It's full of stars!*'

In the novel, therefore, we find no trace of the film's gradual erasure of all signs of human activity and of all ties with the cradle/planet.

We should also note that, originally, the Kubrick–Clarke collaboration was to have the novel accompany the release of the film, which would have borne both their names. The practice of 'novelisation' already existed at the time; the 60s produced novels entitled *La dolce vita* or *À bout de souffle*, which represented the screenplays of these famous films, arranged to varying degrees by their co-editors. Kubrick obliged Clarke to delay the publication of his novel (which was finished before the film), and this seems to have led the publisher to destroy the type of the first edition. But the success of Clarke's book after the film came out, a book that has been reprinted many times since, provided generous compensation to the writer for this mishap.

Elements Removed: Voice-over and Documentary Prologue

The film's release was scheduled for December 1966, taking into account the time that would be needed for the 'tricks', as the special effects were called. The first version of the screenplay intended to show the aliens on screen; they were described as taller than us, with two arms and two legs.

Certain sequences, particularly 'The Dawn of Man', were conceived to be accompanied throughout by a voice-over narrator explaining the action. The sample provided by technical consultant Frederick Ordway makes the skin crawl, so pompous is this narration, which fortunately was eliminated:

> The remorseless drought had lasted now for ten million years, and would not
> end for another million. The reign of the terrible lizards had long since
> passed, but here on the continent which would one day be known as Africa,
> the battle for survival had reached a new climax of ferocity, and the victor
> was not yet in sight.[13]

The film at this stage, and as it was intended to be shown in the cinemas, was to begin with a ten-minute documentary prologue, in 35mm black-and-white. This was shot, and consisted of a montage of interviews with specialists in various fields. Kubrick says he started feeling his prologue was a bad idea sometime towards the end of post-production, after the first screening for the MGM brass in Culver City in early 1968. These interviews subsequently omitted from the film have been transcribed in part in Jerome Agel's book.[14] They involved questions of the uniqueness or plurality of life forms, the peripheral place of man in the universe, the possibility that man might make contact with species outside the solar system, what becomes of religion and belief in God in the light of discoveries about the immensity of the universe (and, among others, the question of whether Judaism is compatible with hypotheses about aliens). The origin of life on earth also arises as a topic, as does the possibility that computers might reach the degree of complexity characteristic of life and the human brain.

The idea at the time was not merely to bring scientific credibility to the film or make a novelised documentary out of it. This prologue provided the basis for the spectacular effects found in the first Cinerama shows: it allowed the film to begin with an image in 'small format' that would dramatise what was to follow by contrast – widescreen, colour and stereo sound. The prologue idea remains present, however, throughout the film, in which each section seems preparatory to the next, right up to the open ending.

Choices in Shooting

Production began during 1965; the budget was set at more than six million dollars, which was very high at the time, and it would end up going four and a half million over. One of Kubrick's obsessions would be the race against the clock with the real landing on the moon. The film was saved, so to speak, by the terrible accident that befell Apollo 1 in 1967, and which delayed plans for the definitive mission to the moon by more than two years.

The title changed to become the one we now know. Kubrick asked expressly that it be pronounced 'two thousand and one', and not, as English usage permits, 'twenty oh one', which did not sound as good to his ears.

The shooting began on 29 December 1965, in the Shepperton studios south-west of London, with the scene of the discovery of the monolith on the moon (only the images of the excavation pit around the object, surrounded by lights – the complete moon terrain, the stars and the earth would be added afterwards). Clarke recalls that no one at that time knew what the moon's surface was like, seen up close. It might well be covered with a thick layer of dust that an astronaut's feet would sink into. He adds that his speculations on the nature of the lunar surface were not too badly contradicted by the actual landing. According to Clarke, the sole indication that *2001* was shot before the Apollo era was the jagged outline of the mountains on the film's moon, because on the real moon the landscape turned out to be much more eroded.

In this brief overview we should note that in the Clavius crater scene, the monolith was made of wood and coated with successive layers of black paint mixed with graphite. For the deeply moving shot of the astronauts' walk down into the excavation pit, in which the camera accompanies them almost as if it were one of them, Kubrick himself manoeuvred the cumbersome Mitchell 65mm camera with the help of two assistants (he would do the same for another memorable shot – the hand-held shot following Bowman on the way to Hal's memory circuits).

In January 1966 the shooting moved to the MGM studios in Borehamwood, a district of offices and small electronics and precision machine factories located some fifteen miles north-west of London. The last crank of the camera occurred before the end of 1966, but then began a laborious phase of post-production, including special effects. That period also saw much hesitation and experimenting and many blind alleys.

By his own account, Kubrick always enjoyed the fullest co-operation of MGM head Robert O'Brien, who supported him in the face of the company's shareholders. No one was able to quarrel with the first script, because there never was a first script. During the shooting, he brought in more and more changes and often incorporated suggestions made by actors. He liked to speak lines of dialogue out loud, finding that this method yielded more natural-sounding dialogue.

For scientific accuracy, he followed the advice of a large number of experts, including Marvin Minsky of MIT, a specialist in artificial intelligence. He also watched every sci-fi film he could, as well as films of any genre that had special-effects sequences. In those days, of course, there were no such things as videocassettes: it was necessary either to procure prints of the films in question or keep on the lookout for their appearance in regular cinemas, under conditions that were not always the best – dubbed soundtracks and faded or chopped-up prints were common.

The director asked the great designer Ken Adam, who had worked on *Dr Strangelove*, to participate on the film, but Adam declined. He was afraid he might not have the time to get sufficiently up to speed on Kubrick's project and on the new technical resources required.

Kubrick perceived a significant problem in the conception of the costumes. He sought to present something that would accurately conform to
what could be imagined of the future, but he also wanted to avoid any
bizarre designs that would distract viewers. Going against the majority of
futuristic sci-fi films made until then, Kubrick chose to present some male
characters in suits and jackets; and we can see that on this point – the
hypothesis that masculine clothing would remain stable through time – history proved him right. For the outfit of the stewardess in zero gravity, he
chose a formula that, although futuristic at the time, was also in style, and
might remind us of certain creations of André Courrèges.

The same goes for music. 'The problem was to find something that
sounded unusual and distinctive but not so unusual as to be distracting.'[15]
Kubrick reported having listened to miles of tape recordings of *musique
concrète* and electronic music to try to find the spirit of the film, but he
sometimes wondered if he should perhaps commission a score from an
important composer, whether a specialist or not in film music. It is notable
that, while writing the screenplay with Clarke, he often listened to Carl
Orff's *Carmina Burana*. Apparently he even contacted Orff in the quest
for an original score, but the German composer, then in his seventies,
declined the honour on account of his age.

The casting was done fairly early on. The principal roles went to Americans, but it seems that the British unions had obtained an agreement that
allowed a number of English actors to be recruited. This could explain why
the voyagers in the Discovery are watching a BBC programme, in which
they are interviewed by one Martin Amer who speaks with a pure English
accent.

Born in Cleveland in 1936, Keir Dullea, chosen for the role of Dave
Bowman, had acted in *David and Lisa* (Frank Perry, 1962, which won a
prize at Venice), *Mail Order Bride*, a Western by Burt Kennedy (1964), *The
Thin Red Line* (Andrew Marton, 1964) – the first filmed version of the
novel by James Jones which inspired Terrence Malick's famous film, *Bunny
Lake Is Missing* (1965) – a little-known Otto Preminger thriller set in
London, and *The Fox* (Mark Rydell, 1967). Later he would play the mar-
quis de Sade in *De Sade* (Cy Endfield and an uncredited Roger Corman,
in a US–West German co-production, 1969), and a number of TV roles,

but his career would not go far. In Peter Hyams's 1984 sequel, *2010*, he makes some brief appearances, like an icon to be trotted out with care.

Little did he know that the role of Bowman would grow into a cinematic legend from which it would subsequently be difficult to escape. At the time of *2001*, he expressed his gratefulness to Kubrick for freeing him from his customary role of 'an introverted, neuter young boy with parent problems, usually my mother'.[16] (In *David and Lisa*, he plays a teenage mental patient with a fear of physical contact.) While one would tend to consider him in *2001* as a passive actor, a puppet in a space suit, he claims much of the credit for what he brought to Dave Bowman: 'I tried to show him as a man without emotional highs and lows – an intelligent, highly trained man, lonely and alienated, not too imaginative.'[17] He also stated that the finished film was only distantly related to the shooting script, in part because a great many of the lines as written in the shooting script were changed during filming and editing.

Gary Lockwood (Frank Poole, Bowman's first mate) was playing secondary roles in films and TV (he appeared in Kazan's masterpiece *Splendor in the Grass*), after a period as a football player – which may have inspired the shadow-boxing scene in *2001*. He was known as the main actor in the 1963–4 TV series *The Lieutenant*. He, too, claims to have invented much of Frank Poole, even if Kubrick had provided some guidelines for the character. In 1969 he went on to play the partner of Anouk Aimée in Jacques Demy's *Model Shop*, whose commercial failure thwarted his career. Thus neither Dullea nor Lockwood became stars, in spite of their prominence in *2001*.

According to the film-maker and writer Andrew Birkin, who was a trainee working on the film at the time, neither Lockwood nor Dullea, struck by the flatness of the lines they had to deliver in the most neutral way possible, was capable of understanding where the director was going with this method: 'they were well paid, so they didn't complain; but both of them thought Kubrick was cracked'.[18]

For the voice of Hal, the first actor to be considered was Nigel Davenport, but his English accent presented a problem for an American computer. Then the American actor Martin Balsam (known for Sidney Lumet's *Twelve Angry Men*, 1957, and Hitchcock's *Psycho*, 1960, as the detective Arbogast) was slated to record Hal. But his voice was deemed too 'emotional', or else (according to Clarke) Balsam himself might have decided not to participate in the film. In any event, Kubrick then turned to the Canadian actor Douglas Rain, who had originally been hired as the voice-over narrator until the narration was scrapped. Rain was a theatre actor who had cut his teeth on Shakespeare; his vocal timbre was much closer to the simultaneously neutral and unctuous quality Kubrick was looking for. He recorded his part in nine and a half hours in the studio, all in a weekend, without having seen a single image from the film and knowing little about the script.

From the beginning, Kubrick scrupulously avoided hiring well-known actors, apparently in order to safeguard the mystery surrounding his film. The intervention of a movie star would necessarily create specific expectations, as well as pre-established associations that might be superimposed on his role.

Geoffrey Unsworth (1915–78), who would later shoot Boorman's *Zardoz* and Bob Fosse's *Cabaret* among others, was *2001*'s director of photography. The shots that were to have special effects added to represent the surface of another world were filmed in the Hebrides in Scotland, over Colorado's Grand Canyon and in Monument Valley. These were done under the supervision of the cinematographer John Alcott, who would go on to be chief operator on *A Clockwork Orange* and *Barry Lyndon*. The images that would provide the setting for the 'Dawn of Man' section were transparencies on large-format film (Ektachrome 10 x 12) brought back from South West Africa by a special team directed by the photographer Robert Watts and production designer Ernie Archer, a team that included the French photographer Pierre Boulat. To get these images, Andrew Birkin, who was sent on location, recounts that Kubrick asked him to arrange, through generously greasing the palms of the local authorities, for the cutting down and transplanting of state-protected thousand-year-old African trees whose forms the director loved, but which he wanted with a different landscape in the background. It was then necessary to destroy the trees to hide the evidence of this shady deal.[19]

These photos for the initial sequence were projected as background on a shooting stage at the Elstree studio, using not the classic rear-projection but a process of front-projection, while the decorators deployed much ingenuity in constructing and lighting a studio set to accommodate and perfectly align the slides.

The conception of the room where Dave Bowman lands at the end went through much revision. At the outset, this was supposed to be a modern-style bedroom, with a telephone that the character would notice was fake. It took some time for the idea of a bedroom in an antique style to emerge.

Models, Production Design and Special Effects

At first the design team headed by Tony Masters envisaged the 'sentinel' in the pyramidal form described in Clarke's story, but visually this did not yield the desired result. 'The tetrahedron didn't look monumental or simple or fundamental. It tended to express diminution more than impressive scale. And there would be people who would think of pyramids.'[20] It was decided to give it the oblong shape with which we are now familiar.

For the motion of spacecraft, which required very exacting frame-by-frame photography to obtain a perfect rendering and matched movements of foreground and background elements, Kubrick chose a costly solution that consisted of filming the models in movement from a great many different angles, so as to have as rich as possible a source of material for editing. After all, how could Kubrick have decided *a priori* on an editing sequence for one type of image – stars and spacecraft rotating or moving – since it did not correspond in any way to usual cases?

In the plot, the secret goal of the Discovery mission (why it is being hidden from the crew is one mystery among many in the screenplay) is to reach the spot from where the signal to the monolith was transmitted. Early in production, this was supposed to be the planet Saturn. But Saturn's famous rings made it very complicated to construct believable models, and after months of effort Kubrick decided to return to the initial idea, Jupiter, the largest planet of the solar system, which like Saturn possesses several moons.

It is noteworthy that, in the finished film, Jupiter is depicted unobtrusively, with no insistence on its famous red spot.[21] The various planets of *2001* resemble one another somewhat, and are not visually marked by huge differences, to the extent that some critics and spectators have become confused at times. Earth, far from being shown as weather satellites have obliged us to see it – as a blue globe peppered with cloud cover – is a uniformly white and luminous sphere in the film, on which one cannot distinguish clearly the shapes of the continents. The scrupulous editor of the shot breakdown published in the French film journal *L'Avant-Scène*, in the final scene with the Star Child, is not sure whether it is earth or the moon she sees opposite the foetus, and she is honest enough to admit this (we do see another celestial body behind, however, which has to be the moon). We 'know', because of the accumulated documentation on the genesis of the film and the different states of its screenplay, that this can be no other than the earth – but are we sure we see it?

The audience at the time that *2001* was made did not then know exactly what was meant by special effects, and the term used was 'tricks', sometimes used with a naïve and puerile connotation. Even among science-fiction aficionados, there was as yet no culture of special effects in themselves, and thus, aside from professional magazines like *American Cinematographer*, not many behind-the-scenes articles about the fabrication of the visuals of *2001*. The 1970 book by Jerome Agel called *The Making of Kubrick's 2001* revealed many of the secrets that went into the making of the film, and supplied illustrative photos, but this documentation occupies only a small part of what is primarily a collection of essays, interviews and reviews.[22]

It is not my intention here to dwell on the 'making of'; for that the reader can consult Agel, Schwam, Bizony and various Kubrick biographies. A film has never been made in the abstract, and the technical limitations of the time obviously dictated the awkwardness of certain shots: for example, where the camera is immobile while we see space bodies move. But we would be wrong to see in these technical limitations the cause of the choices Kubrick made. What is important is the universe he was able to create out of and in spite of these limitations, a universe whose sense of reality and poetry surpasses its technical foundations.

'Space operas' before Kubrick often inspired parody for their unconvincing models. Rockets, planets and cities often brought to mind the tiny models that they really were – not to mention the monsters and other creatures. Kubrick attacked the problem from this direction: he constructed fairly large models with painstaking detail throughout. The models were filmed, animated and lit with great care for the unforgiving eye of the 65mm Panavision camera. The model for the space station, for instance, measured over six feet in diameter. Kubrick's desire for visual credibility and for scientific truth led him to reproduce exact views of the moon or Jupiter based on the latest images then available.

In order to create the abstract imagery of the Star Gate sequence, Kubrick employed several means. He jealously guarded the secret of several of his special effects, and proudly claimed in the credits, 'special photographic effects by Stanley Kubrick'. For other effects, he called on Roy Naisbitt and a camera system on rails inspired by the work of the experimental film-maker John Whitney and conceived by the brilliant Douglas Trumbull. This is the system called Slitscan, which creates the visual 'corridor' effect so notable in this sequence.

According to Jean-Pierre Bouyxou, the Italian director Antonio Margheriti, born in 1931 (who worked in various genres, from sci-fi and epics to Westerns, sometimes under the pseudonym of Anthony Dawson), collaborated anonymously in the preparation of the American special effects. 'Then I made a film for Metro, and Kubrick began shooting. In the end, the finished film doesn't look anything like the initial project, it lost much of its meaning ... 2001 is a beautiful film, but too intellectual.'[23]

The film's imagery drew from all sorts of sources: op-art painting, architectural projects, printed circuits, electron microphotographs. Chemical reactions were created and then filmed with a macro lens. For a long time Kubrick doggedly tried to create credible aliens, which in some phases took on the elongated look of Giacometti sculptures, in an unwritten tradition that is difficult to trace, but which is still respected by numerous movies that have 'good' extraterrestrials, such as James Cameron's *The Abyss* (1989).

Ultimately, *2001* chose not to render the aliens visible, but it was not for lack of trying. Again, the absences on which *2001* seems to be founded are not abstract decisions made at the outset and rigidly adhered to. *2001* is truly a work created through the process of trial and error.

The refusal to show the extraterrestrials, the visual embodiment of which would have constituted the highlight of the film and justified its structure, disappointed crew members such as Con Pederson, who had spent many months working on this complex problem. Some people still believe they have spotted shots of aliens in the 'trip' sequence.

Filming with Actors

For live-action shots with actors, one of the highlighted sets is the Discovery's giant centrifuge, that creates artificial gravity for the ship's residents. Many are the anecdotes regarding the dimensions of this great wheel, the dangers it created (certain objects forgotten on the floor, despite precautions taken, became projectiles when the wheel was set turning like a Ferris wheel at three miles per hour), the ingenious systems of mirrors used to film certain shots, and the closed-circuit television set-up that Kubrick was among the first to use to watch the shooting from a remote location.

The director also made use of enormous numbers of Polaroid pictures (also new at the time) to document filmed shots and to use for reference in continuity.

The high luminosity dominating the film results in part from Kubrick's decision to open the aperture to the maximum for interior sets as well as models. Objects in space and the walls of the sets thus seem irradiated by light. As far as possible, light comes from sources present in the set itself, either in the ceiling (the lobby of the Orbiter Hilton) or beneath the floor (the period bedroom).

The sole eyewitness account of the shooting of the film (which was otherwise kept secret), by Jeremy Bernstein, confirms that Kubrick had in mind a film that would avoid conventional dramatisation and acting. There is a description of a simple scene that did not survive the final edit, in which Dave awakens in his 'hibernaculum'. 'Just open your eyes. Let's not have any stirring, yawning, and rubbing,' ordered Kubrick.[24] It was Kubrick himself who on the sound stage fed Hal's line to Keir Dullea: 'Good morning. What do you want for breakfast?' For the shooting of other scenes, the assistant director Derek Cracknell was the temporary voice of Hal, and in his Cockney accent supplied lines to Dullea like 'My mind is going.'

From the same essay we learn that the music played on set during the filming of the scene where Poole is training and boxing, and which would help Lockwood to choreograph his movements, was a Chopin waltz chosen by Kubrick. (In the finished film, this became an adagio by Khacha-turian, carefully chosen and edited with respect to the image so as not to give the sense that the character is moving to the music or that he hears it – this is itself contrary to the original idea.) Like Sergio Leone, Kubrick was an expert at this practice, as old as silent cinema, which consists of getting the actors in the mood and in rhythm by having music played on the set.

Certain scenes were expressly written and shot not so much to advance the plot, but to depict a world without gravity. For example, there is the scene of the flight attendant walking on the ceiling during the Aries's flight to the moon. It may be that for today's viewers this spectacular imagery (a classic of special-effects cinema, of which we find a dancing version by Fred Astaire in Stanley Donen's 1951 film *Royal Wedding*) is fairly musty, but it retains its formal function, which is to vividly establish different time and space dimensions.

For the scenes of the 'Dawn of Humanity', apart from a brief shot with real baby chimpanzees seen examining a bone without making use of it (in order to underscore the evolutionary split that is about to occur between two closely related species), the apemen are played by mime actors and dancers in ape suits. One of them is even credited at the end: Dan Richter plays the leader of the ape clan, the one who works out a use for the bone. It was necessary to recruit actors with very skinny arms and legs and nar-row hips, so they would not look fat in the costumes. Tongues and teeth were false, of course, only the actors' real eyes remained visible. When the film came out, the apes appeared so real that chief make-up artist Stuart Freeborn was understandably disappointed to see the 1968 Oscar for make-up go to John Chambers for another bunch of anthropoids – in *Planet of the Apes*, much more obviously portrayed by actors (the latter apes spoke, too).

Almost all the scenes of this episode were studio-shot. Only the scene where the ape leader discovers the tool was shot outside, against the back-ground of a real English sky. One of the main reasons for the decision not to shoot on location was concern for a unified lighting scheme. John Alcott recounts that the opening scene was to unfold in the very weak light of dawn, and to do it right would have taken months of filming on location in Africa.

During the entire period of filming, as I have said, Kubrick continued to make changes. For example, for the scene of the Regency bedroom, it was only at the last moment that he would hit on the brilliant idea to have Dave age through cutting:

> The ending was altered shortly before shooting it. In the original, there was
> no transformation of Bowman. He just wandered around the room and
> finally saw the artifact. But this didn't seem like it was satisfying enough, or
> interesting enough, and we constantly searched for ideas until we finally came
> up with the ending as you see it.[25]

Editing: Doubts, Additions and Cuts

At the editing stage, which went on for a considerable time, Kubrick reportedly tried out many solutions and many different musical pieces, and had incessant doubts about the final form the film would take. He continued to make changes until – and even after – the first screening.[26] The journalist Jeremy Bernstein admits that he was totally surprised upon seeing the finished film, and Keir Dullea and others close to the production had the same reaction.

For example, according to the original script, the Star Child was supposed to set off detonations of nuclear weapons around the earth in outer space. This was eliminated in the final cut. In fact, the film no longer contains anything to identify the first space objects that we see as bombs, even though when they were designed they were conceived and then filmed as military satellites.

The script also included several sequences or dialogue lines essential to understanding the story, and whose removal in the editing stage made the story much more enigmatic. For example, in the Discovery, Poole expressed his suspicions to Hal in these terms: '[There is] something about this mission that we weren't told. Something the rest of the crew [the hibernating astronauts] know and that you know.'[27] Hal answers that he cannot say anything about this. After this line was taken out, the con-

nection between the hibernation of the three astronauts and the mystery
of the monolith became completely incomprehensible.[28]

The rejection of the voice-over narration and the cutting of certain
scenes created many other misunderstandings, or one-way interpretations,
which ended up by adding to the film's mystery.

For example, at the screenplay stage, it is clear that when the monolith
begins sending out a signal that pierces the astronauts' helmets, this is
because it is the lunar dawn: the lunar night is the equivalent of fourteen
days on earth and the monolith was exhumed in the intervening time, so
that the sun is hitting it for the first time in four million years. But as this
event happens to occur while they are getting ready to photograph the
monolith, for all we know the monolith is emitting its electromagnetic
screech in protest against being captured on film.

Nor is it told to us anywhere in the finished film that the antenna unit
of which Hal announces the imminent failure is essential for all communication with earth. Furthermore, the purely objective manner in which
this matter is treated by everyone (Dave, Frank, Hal, Mission Control on
earth) makes us think that this is a routine incident – which leads us to
watch with eyes more contemplative than panic-stricken the manoeuvres
that are executed to repair the AE-35 unit and test it. Did Kubrick
'measure' and 'master' these effects? Many factors demonstrate that
nothing could be less certain.

Today we can only imagine the perplexity of many of the first cinema-
goers in 1968 – of whom I was one – when faced with this extremely
elliptical, incoherent film, even if it was fascinating. Today's spectator sees
the work quite differently, influenced by its history, the explanations fur-
nished by Clarke's novel and a series of 'revelations' made after the fact,
a whole tradition of exegesis that was handed down, particularly by critics
and the press, and that constitutes a common and reassuring background
of understanding, even for those who have not read the novel. To watch
2001 as it was seen on its release implies attempting to forget this tradition,
an almost impossible task. Nevertheless, this does not prevent the film,
although overlaid with all these commentaries, from retaining its mystery
for those who discover it today.

Before the premiere Kubrick made another series of cuts, all towards the same general purpose: he wished to end up with a film that severed its ties with the earth and life as we know it. The scenes taken out at this stage were as follows:

- A scene in which Floyd, in the space station, uses the videophone, on which he has just called his daughter, to reach Macy's department store and order the bushbaby doll the little girl requested for her birthday. This scene apparently showed some fleeting images of earth. I have not seen a single image of it.
- Scenes showing the life and activities of the Clavius moon base. One production still reproduced in the book by Piers Bizony gives us an idea of this. In a rather surrealist domed paradise, at once idyllic and synthetic, long-haired little girls (including two of Kubrick's three daughters, Anya and Katharina) are grouped around a tiny artificial pond strewn with water lilies, and are painting at easels. In the background Floyd and the other conference participants, in suits with badges, look like convention delegates taking a coffee break. Other shots show shops, and children (born on base) running around.

    This deletion, and the fact that Kubrick preferred to go directly to Floyd's speech behind closed doors, now makes the moon landing just beforehand seem repetitious with regard to the sequence of the Orion flight. It brings no new narrative element, and does not announce a new setting. It does no more than become part of the film as an extension of the first images of space flight.
- Finally, on the Discovery, Kubrick cut shots of a ping-pong table, a piano, a shower – all things that remind us of life on earth.

It is with this first version of about two hours and forty minutes that an invitation-only preview was held on 1 April 1968, at the Capitol Theater in New York. This screening was apparently received coldly – 'too long, boring, disjointed, incomprehensible', comments that Kubrick attributed both to his film's originality and to the fact that the audience consisted mostly of people over 35. He would be counting on the under-35 audience to make the film a success.[29] He was none the less influenced by this reaction, and took it into account when he cut out an additional nineteen minutes.

According to various sources, these cuts were as follows:

• Some shots from the 'Dawn of Man' sequence (I think the wonderful cut, simultaneously in both sound and image, that connects the image of apes eating meat to a savage struggle between two clans could have been the result of one of these cuts);

• Some shots of Poole jogging in the centrifuge, a segment that was shortened despite all the work this particular scene had entailed;

• An entire scene of several shots in which Dave looks for the new antenna part in a storage area;

• A scene where Hal cuts radio communication between the Discovery and Poole's pod before killing him (a scene that motivates a line Bowman addresses to Hal on this subject – the line stayed in the film and thus is unclear);

• Some of the shots of Poole's spacewalk before he is killed.

It was also at this point that Kubrick introduced an important explanatory addition: the subjective shot of the monolith, in low-angle, inserted into the scene where the ape pauses with the bone he is about to use as an instrument. Many spectators had not made the connection between the discovery of the tool and the appearance of the monolith just before. (In my analysis of the film, the fact that this shot was added *in extremis* does not lead me to consider it differently from the others. The work is the work.)

Kubrick would later declare:

> I made all the cuts in *2001* and at no one's request. I had not had an opportunity to see the film complete with music, sound effects, etc., until about a week before it opened, and it does take a few runnings to decide finally how long things should be, especially scenes which do not have narrative advancement as their guideline. Most of the scenes that were cut were impressions of things.[30]

The Story of an Abandoned Score

Let us turn to the episode of Alex North's abandoned score.

Alex North, the American son of Russian immigrants, had been the composer for Kubrick's 1960 film *Spartacus*. He was also known for films like *A Streetcar Named Desire* (Elia Kazan, 1951, exemplifying a new tendency for jazz in American film music at the time), John Huston's *The Misfits*, 1961 (North would work for Huston again towards the end of his life), and Herman Mankiewicz's ambitious 1964 epic, *Cleopatra*.

We know that *Dr Strangelove*, Kubrick's previous film, had already taken a step towards abandoning traditional film scoring by integrating several songs *in extenso* alongside an intentionally schematic score by Laurie Johnson.

According to Robert Townson, Kubrick initially intended to use classical music excerpts, and it was MGM that preferred an original score and suggested to the director that he work with North again.[31] On being contacted, North accepted with enthusiasm, not just because of his admiration for Kubrick, but also because of the prospect of working on a film that had so little dialogue. 'What a dreamy assignment, after *Who's Afraid of Virginia Woolf*, loaded with dialogue.'[32]

In December 1967, North and Kubrick met in London, but Kubrick admitted to the composer that he intended to retain at least some of the temp(orary) track that had been used in the preceding months. Among others, they were the Scherzo from Mendelssohn's *A Midsummer Night's Dream* and Ralph Vaughan Williams's 'Sinfonia Antarctica' for the Cosmic Trip sequence.[33] The practice of the temp track consists of editing a piece of pre-existing music to a scene so as to find the scene's inner rhythm, before the new, original score is composed. Owing to the peculiar capacity for music to 'grow into' the film with repetition and time, the director often acquires a fondness for the temp track, and more than one has requested music from their composers, to the latters' chagrin, that is barely more than a pastiche of the temporary excerpts.

North apparently argued, with good reason, that it would be better to let him compose the score as a whole, in order to avoid a patchwork of musical styles. Besides, he was already hard at work musically formulating what Kubrick sought in each scene. The composer had to work rapidly, as is often the case in film scoring, with the aid of orchestrator Henry Brandt. In particular, he proposed new pieces to substitute for *Zarathustra* and for the Scherzo from *A Midsummer Night's Dream* (which in the final film is the 'Blue Danube' Waltz).

When North had composed only part of the planned cues, Kubrick notified him that he no longer needed any supplementary music and that he was going to use sounds of breathing for the remainder of the film (it must be realised that his status as the film's producer allowed him to maintain absolute control over the music).

Nevertheless, not until the first public screening in New York in April 1968 did North realise that the film did not contain a single note of his score. His shock was as one might expect. It was not casualness or indifference but rather, I suspect, profound embarrassment on Kubrick's part, along with profound doubts about his own decisions, that might explain his failure to notify North – who had at least been paid.

During the 80s, in the context of a series of rerecordings of great scores by North, Robert Townson suggested recording the *2001* score under the direction of Jerry Goldsmith. This music had previously gone unheard and unknown, although the composer had dipped into it for his Third Symphony and for other, later film scores such as *Dragonslayer* in 1981. North died in 1991, knowing at least that his score would be reborn, and the recording was made in January 1993. The recording reveals to us a rich, symphonic, appropriately modern piece that overwhelms the listener who dreams of the 'other film' this would have created.

Reception

The buzz of press releases and interviews on the release of *2001* put the spotlight on its concern for scientific and futurological accuracy; in terms of the values of the time, the publicity implicitly focused on its character as an adult science-fiction film. The challenge was to convince a wider audience than the usual specialised sci-fi buffs – fervent, but limited in number – and to fight against the reputation of puerility that was usually associated with the genre.[34] The press releases also developed a highly optimistic vision of the 'year 2000': 'Transportation by ballistic missile will reduce travel to any point on the globe to under an hour. Domestic robots will do all the tedious work while the lady of the house does her shopping by videophone. ... Cancer, senility and mental illness will no longer exist,' says the French press kit.

We know what has become of these predictions. But rather than smile smugly, let us think of today's predictions, and plan to meet in thirty years' time to see what has become of them!

Another tactic of the publicity documents was to stop in its tracks any criticism focused on the unbelievability of the film's contents. For example, for the scene where the stewardess is walking upside down, the press release alludes to a new material called Velcro, developed for space. The release also affirms, to justify the scene where Dave Bowman has to re-enter the Discovery manually, that it is indeed possible for a human to survive several seconds in a vacuum; it furthermore states that science will soon make hibernation by humans possible. And, of course, it assures us that with progress, computers will soon be perfected to 'behave like conscious beings'.

The critical and public reception of the film was quite divided. The film intrigued and polarised; some critics even left during the intermission, while others were perplexed about the meaning of the ending. Fellini sent a telegram expressing 'his emotion, his enthusiasm', John Lennon declared that he was watching it once a week. The film sparked discussion, and left no one indifferent. In any case, the long-term box-office receipts were excellent. Renata Adler of the *New York Times* voiced her reservations about a 'very complicated, languid movie ... it is somewhere between hypnotic and immensely boring'.[35] She hailed the beauty of its special effects, but emphasised that the work accumulates disparate plot lines without reconciling them in a meaningful way. The slabs, the period bedroom and Dave's ageing 'are simply left there like a Rorschach'.[36] The most frequent complaints were those that found the film cold and confused, characters nonentities, dialogue meaningless and technique too foregrounded at the expense of emotion.

In *Harper's*, Pauline Kael described Kubrick's work as the irresponsible whim of a spoiled child, who is amusing himself inconsequentially with the big toy of technique. For Kael, this is 'the biggest amateur movie of them all, complete even to the amateur-movie obligatory scene – the director's little daughter (in curls) telling daddy what kind of present she wants'.[37]

According to Vincent LoBrutto, this criticism particularly wounded the director, which is completely understandable, for it is always very easy for a critic to zero in on the particular moment when its auteur – and why shouldn't he? – is simply *enjoying himself* in the midst of a work that is ambitious, courageous and with gigantic human import. At the same time, Kael was certainly not wrong in directing attention to the childlike spirit that pervades the film. It is only that she seems to have seen in this a weakness, where I see greatness.

On the other hand, Penelope Gilliatt in the *New Yorker* extolled *2001* as a magnificent film, and she attributed some of its surprises to Kubrick's humour. For her, the 'Blue Danube' Waltz contributes to evoke a civilisation in *2001* that has 'the brains of a nuclear physicist and the sensibility of an airline hostess smiling through an oxygen-mask demonstration'.[38] In a remarkable essay, she noted with insight the reign of routine, the feeling of affective isolation, the absence between characters of any sense of sexual interest or friendship, the emptiness of family communication, the recurrent theme of birthdays (Floyd's daughter, Frank Poole), and the clinical and frighteningly modern quality of the hibernating astronauts' deaths. She underscored the ambiguity of one part of the film: like the god Siva, a single thing can signify both destruction and creation.

2001 was nominated for four Academy Awards, but received only the Oscar for special visual effects. The critically anointed film that year was *Oliver!*, the musical by Carol Reed based on Dickens's *Oliver Twist*. In the UK, *2001* won the prize for best artistic direction, due to Tony Masters, Harry Lange and Ernest Archer.

It turned out that *2001* was a film people were going to see many times, and its myth began to emerge. In France, the book by Jean-Paul Dumont and Jean Monod with the intriguing title *Le Foetus astral* took inspiration from Claude Lévi-Strauss and did a structural analysis of Kubrick's film, contributing further towards solidifying its reputation on the Continent. In 1993, a jury of critics for *Sight and Sound* included *2001* in the Top Ten of film history.

The film opened in France in October 1968. In Paris, two cinemas were showing it in 70mm: the Cinérama (which later became the Théâtre de l'Empire and is used today for public tapings of television shows), for the

English-language print with subtitles,[39] and, for the print dubbed in French, the Gaumont-Palace (a cinema legendary for its organ, but now no longer in existence).

The French dub was supervised by the director Henri Verneuil, and it is the voice of Jean-Louis Trintignant that substitutes (quite well, we may add) for Douglas Rain in the role of Hal's voice[40] – which for French audiences was rebaptised Carl, acronym for 'Centre analytique de recherche et de liaison', Analytic Centre for Research and Communication. Rather ingeniously, in the scene of the computer's death, Hal was made to sing the popular tune 'Au clair de la lune' to replace 'A Bicycle Made for Two'. The lyrics, beyond their allusion to the heavens (moonlight), resonate nicely in the scene: 'My candle has gone out, I have no more flame …'.

My own first viewing of Kubrick's film was in English at the Empire. But I arrived during the intermission – this was still during the period when Parisian cinemas ran movies over and over again, with no breathing space in between. Since then, I have never stopped picking up where I left off in the film and then seeking the way out …

Notes

1   Arthur C. Clarke, 'The Sentinel', reprinted in Schwam, pp. 17–26.
2   Ibid., p. 15.
3   [Clarke was president of the British Interplanetary Society 1946–7 and 1950–3. – Translator.]
4   Goimard, 'Une Odyssée formelle'.
5   The amusing theory that holds that this name was found by taking the three letters that precede IBM in the alphabet has frequently been disclaimed by Clarke and Kubrick. It is no more than a coincidence: Hal is the acronym of *H*euristic and *Al*gorithmic, the two principal computer systems. Hal's name in the French version of *2001*, by the way, is Carl.
6   Kubrick, quoted in the unpaginated 96-page photo insert of Jerome Agel's *The Making of Kubrick's 2001*.
7   Kubrick had filmed *Spartacus* in Super Technirama 70mm, to be distributed in CinemaScope. His plan was to shoot *2001* in the 1.85:1 Panavision format.

8 Jeremy Bernstein, 'Beyond the Stars' (*New Yorker*, 1966), in Schwam, p. 28.

9 Clarke, quoted by Bernstein, ibid., p. 28.

10 Ibid.

11 Similarly, the 1959 movie adaptation of Jules Verne's *Journey to the Center of the Earth*, directed by Henry Levin, introduces a woman character sharing the heroes' 'odyssey' who was not in the Verne original.

12 Original press release of 23 February 1965, courtesy Piers Bizony, in Schwam, p. 142.

13 From Frederick I. Ordway, scientific and technical consultant, reprinted in Schwam, p. 126.

14 Agel, pp. 27–57.

15 Bernstein, 'How About a Little Game?', in Schwam, p. 86.

16 Keir Dullea, quoted in Agel, p. 313.

17 Ibid., loc. cit.

18 Andrew Birkin, interviewed by the magazine *Studio* (Paris), transcribed by Christophe d'Yvoire, no. 144, April 1999, pp. 118–19.

19 Ibid., loc. cit.

20 Special photographic effects supervisor Con Pederson, quoted in Agel, p. 76.

21 One has only to compare this Jupiter with the one in Peter Hyams's *2010*.

22 Much of Agel's book, long out of print, has reappeared in 2000 in the collection selected by Schwam, *The Making of 2001: A Space Odyssey*. This latter volume includes essays by Piers Bizony, Alexander Walker and Simson Garfinkel.

23 Quoted in Bouyxou, *La Science-fiction au cinéma*, p. 469.

24 Bernstein, in Schwam, p. 89.

25 Agel, p. 157.

26 Kubrick's famous perfectionism did not extend to a perfect and untouchable screenplay or fixed shooting script but, on the contrary, allowed freedom for improvisation and spontaneous ideas. *2001*'s dialogue was written and rewritten from one day to the next, and Kubrick loved actors like Peter Sellers and Jack Nicholson precisely because of their tendency to improvise and try new things on the set.

27 Testimony of Frederick Ordway, scientific and technical consultant on
    2001, reprinted in Schwam, p. 128.

28 I need hardly say that in these story 'holes' there is neither error nor any
    particular virtue. They simply become part and parcel of the film in its
    final form. All normative approaches to the screenplay are foreign to me.

29 Interview with Maurice Rapf, quoted in Agel, p. 169.

30 Interview with Maurice Rapf (?) in Agel, p. 170. (Much of Agel's book is
    poorly documented, including the source of these remarks.)

31 Robert Townson, 'The Odyssey of Alex North', liner notes for the CD of
    North's score, Varese I–AB 19–87 (1993).

32 Alex North, in Schwam, p. 129.

33 This work by the English composer is itself inspired in large part by
    Vaughan Williams's own score for a travel documentary. Similarly,
    North would later use music from his rejected *2001* score for a concert
    work.

34 The science-fiction audience is one of the best educated and the least
    superficial there is. They are not numerous, but have played a crucial
    role in the continuing development of the genre and in creating its
    culture.

35 Renata Adler, 'We'll Get this Info to You Just As …' (*New York Times*,
    1 July, 1968), reprinted in Schwam, p. 147.

36 Ibid., p. 148.

37 *Harper's Bazaar*, 1969; reprinted in Schwam, p. 144.

38 'After Man' (*New Yorker*, 1968), reprinted in Agel, p. 210.

39 Bought by the Société Française de Production, the refurbished
    cinema was for a long time the setting for a programme featuring
    Cardinal Jacques Martin, on France's second national channel. In the
    50s and 60s the theatre had shown the first Cinerama films in
    France. The popularity of American Cinerama on an avenue on
    Paris's Right Bank led to the birth of a competing cinema on the
    Left Bank that adopted an equivalent Russian process,
    KinoPanorama. The two opposing blocs could be found everywhere
    then!

40 Trintignant would lend his voice much later to another brain-creature, in
    Marc Caro and Jean-Pierre Jeunet's *City of Lost Children*, where his

familiar inflections were easily recognised by French audiences. Apparently Caro and Jeunet attempted, in a film that I find uneven yet rich, to 'renew' the codes of the 'hidden voice' by giving it a more familiar accent.

Chapter Two
Context

Three years in the making and released in 1968, *2001* was strikingly situated in a rich contextual web. What follows is an overview of some aspects of its historical context, its general cultural context and a more specifically filmic context.

Historical Context: the Space Race and the Cold War

The 60s mark the beginning of the slow thaw in the Cold War, punctuated by crises of greater or lesser gravity, such as the Soviet Union's installation of missiles in Cuba in 1962 when Kennedy and Khruschev brought the world to the brink of nuclear conflict. The world's two superpowers, the United States and the Soviet Union, engaged in a 'race' for the first moon landing, which was to occur in 1969, a year after the release of *2001*. In unpredictable and fortunate ways, the space race, marked by a great number of launchings and missions on both sides, took on the air of sport and, as such, allowed the two powers to sublimate some of the political tension and even to undertake collaborations that symbolised a desire for peace.

It was the Russians who, to their great pride and to American consternation, had sent the first satellite in history, Sputnik 1, into space in October 1957. The United States answered with Explorer 1 in January 1958. It was likewise a Russian, Yuri Gagarin, who flew the first manned space mission (after several flights with animals) on 12 April 1961. Several unmanned rockets revolved around, landed on, or crashed on the moon, before 20 July 1969 when the American Neil Armstrong walked on lunar soil for the first time. This success was the crowning finale to the Apollo programme, launched in 1960 and vigorously supported by President Kennedy. The astronauts on that mission would think more than once about *2001* and its monolith.

When Kubrick began *2001* in 1965, the two global powers were accelerating the space race to warp speed, and everyone on the planet assumed it would continue. The year 2001 seemed quite reasonable then as a date by which we would have regular earth-to-moon flights and huge inhabited bases on the moon. The film's story gives us to understand that these bases had been operational for some time by 2001 – so as I begin writing this book in 1998, they should already be there!

Why hasn't any of this actually occurred, and why is the world of *2001* now no longer our immediate future, but rather one of the many parallel universes that science fiction inevitably leaves in its wake?

Certainly, there were further expeditions (the last manned moon landing was back in 1972), but various factors have considerably slowed what is called 'the conquest of space'. Among the contributing factors were energy crises, the 'back to the earth' movement to save the planet (the sinking of the oiler *Amoco-Cadiz* in 1967 raised the world's ecological consciousness), several dramatic accidents (such as the 1970 Apollo 13 incident, which later became the subject of the Ron Howard movie with Tom Hanks, and the death of three Russian cosmonauts during a landing in 1971) and the waning of public interest. This last factor played a significant role, since the manned flights had a mostly symbolic function. They were much more costly than unmanned flights and, scientifically speaking, less interesting (a remote-controlled robot like Sojourner on Mars could accomplish many more tasks). The awe people felt in viewing and reviewing images of men on the moon or in space slowly turned into habit, and from there to indifference. By then the financing of manned missions, justified more by prestige than by immediate scientific interest, became difficult. Numerous politicians pressured their government to spend public money in better ways.[1]

So the Russians gave up on moon landings but, starting with the Salyut programme, turned their efforts to manned space stations, sometimes with long-term sojourns for the occupants. (It is significant that Tarkovsky's 1972 film *Solaris*, the Soviet cinema's response to *2001*, takes place almost entirely in an orbiting space station.)

The 'conquest' of outer space in the period of the Russo-American competition of the 60s nevertheless created, through endless TV replays, an entire repertoire of televisual imagery of space launches and zero gravity, and *2001* drew on this image bank. The viewers of 1968 had seen and heard, in fuzzy black-and-white pictures and static-filled radio recordings, the floating astronauts that Kubrick would now present to them in 70mm, colour and stereo sound.

The 'conquest' also provided the occasion for symbolic gestures in the direction of peace, as I have said: information exchanges, official trips by astronauts into the opposing camp, the 1968 signing of an agreement by forty-two countries regarding the matter of space rescues. But the threat of a nuclear war ignited by one of the two powers – which was the subject of the brilliant Voltairean farce *Dr Strangelove* – remained present in the public consciousness and in actual fact. We need to know how to read it beneath the surface in *2001*, for it figured importantly in the original screenplay. In a *Playboy* interview at the time of the film's release, Kubrick cautioned readers about the danger of thinking that there was any less risk of nuclear war because of the situation that was being called détente.[2]

Another immediate effect of the space missions was to put outer space as it was 'conquered' into a more relative perspective; the world became more concretely aware of the real dimensions of outer space. No matter how much progress we made in exploring our solar system, we came to understand that the solar system is a mere speck in the universe.

In the much longer run, human travel into space now seemed destined to continue – perhaps it was inevitable, motivated by the exhaustion of the earth's resources, the eventual extinction of the sun and humanity's irrepressible urge to explore. Independent of our calendar relation to the temporal setting of *2001*, the perspectives opened up by Kubrick's film are therefore not about to narrow or fade with time.

Cultural Context: Pop and Psychedelic Culture in the 60s

On the release of *2001*, one of the most widely commented on, and then legendary, sequences was the voyage 'beyond the infinite', which became known as the 'Star Gate' or 'cosmic trip' sequence. 'Trip' is a keyword of 60s culture, even in France where it is used without being translated: it designates a sort of initiation voyage, usually undertaken with the aid of drugs and music. Grooving to a Pink Floyd record, accompanied perhaps by a joint, can constitute a trip. This is distinct from the New Age culture of the 80s and 90s, where meditative experiences are associated with the return to an ancestral culture, and often carrying neo-pagan, neo-animist, even neo-fascist connotations. Nor did ideological/ecological themes such as the idea of a defiled Mother Earth (not to be confused with the real ecological cause itself) have the force they have since taken on.

Sixties culture talked more about seeking consciousness-raising experiences, which would lead to sensory voyages taken as symbolic of contact with the cosmos. The theme of space and weightlessness is also strongly present in some pop music of the era, and also in the way it was spoken of – for example, in French categories such as 'space music' or music to trip on (*musique spatiale*, *musique pour planer*). It was natural at the time for the *Playboy* journalist to ask Kubrick if he took LSD. Kubrick replied that drugs are not for artists, since they cause a sense of satisfaction before you have done all the work, then kill the critical spirit and make anything look beautiful and interesting.

Rock concerts were often occasions for audiovisual experiments in sound and light (remember the 'light shows' that were part and parcel of concerts). Electro-acoustic music such as Pierre Henry's 'Le Voyage' ('The Trip', 1963), based on the Tibetan *Book of the Dead*, the taste for the sonorities of the Indian music of Ravi Shankar and Vilayat Khan – such was a European cultural context in which the word *space*, with all its connotations, played a major role. And *2001*, in the way it culminates in a splendid audiovisual 'trip', makes sense in this context.

It is interesting to note that the film's original publicity campaign highlighted technology and science in both words and visuals, but this strategy quickly changed course when the industry took notice of the film's reception as a 'trip'. The press releases thus changed their tune to exploit this dimension: it was a film 'for grooving, not understanding', a 'psychedelic experience' (*Time*), the 'ultimate trip' (*Christian Science Monitor*).

Cinematic Context

2001 represents an event that influenced many films to follow, but also that was indebted to much that came before. It is a milestone in film history, and for this reason I shall discuss its legacy at much greater length in a later chapter.

Science-fiction Films before *2001*

Before *2001*, science fiction had produced many excellent works, not just enjoyable for their 'naïveté' (a relative notion, for Kubrick's film itself could easily be considered 'naïve' if reduced to its storyline). Of these let us mention *Metropolis* (Fritz Lang, 1926), *Invasion of the Body Snatchers* (Don Siegel, 1955), *The Incredible Shrinking Man* (Jack Arnold, 1957), *The Time Machine* (George Pal, 1960), *Village of the Damned* (Wolf Rilla, 1961), *The Damned* (Joseph Losey, 1961), *La Jetée* (Chris Marker, 1962) and *Quatermass and the Pit* (Roy Ward Baker, 1967).[3]

The genre of science fiction, when not reduced to the sole domain of future worlds, covers several subgenres, among which are the following:

1. *The story of the mad or overreaching scientist*, whose experiments create a synthetic woman or a monstrous man. This story's pedigree dates back to nineteenth-century literature (Mary Shelley, Robert Louis Stevenson, Villiers de l'Isle-Adam, and so on) and has inspired innumerable films. So Hal and Frankenstein's monster have more than one thing in common.

   Hal the computer, who has many predecessors in science-fiction literature that is full of intelligent super-machines regulating the life of a city,[4] actually inherits the double legacy of the Golem and the Robot. The Robot is often shown as a creature overpowering its creator and turning against him – just as man himself, as Prometheus, turns against his Creator. But the computer, often given visual form in the 60s as a whole battery of machines, is also a modern incarnation of the oracle; this is how Welles represents it in his 1962 science-fiction-like adaptation of Kafka's *Trial*.

   The most famous robot of the silver screen before the 60s was a benevolent metallic fellow named Robby, the star of *Forbidden Planet* (Fred McLeod Wilcox, 1956). This film, naïve though it might seem to us today, was long considered one of the more intelligent works of the science-fiction cinema and, before *2001*, was one of the rare sci-fi films to enjoy a respectable budget allowing for both colour and Cinema-Scope. The planet in question, on which Dr Morbius (a character distantly related to *The Tempest*'s Prospero) has settled, was formerly home to a highly evolved civilisation called the Krells. These people had destroyed themselves by constructing a machine that made wishes come true; it unleashed the destructive forces of their unconscious minds. The anti-Promethean warning message of *Forbidden Planet* (do not build machines that will destroy you, and do not forget that within you lies a sleeping monster) is reprised by *2001*, where we again come upon the motif of the machine gone dangerously awry. But we should note that *2001* takes this theme still further. The computer revolts but is defeated; then the man is put into the care of a species with more highly evolved technology, which transfigures him.

2. *Extraterrestrial invasions or visitations*, flying saucers and Martians, often hostile but sometimes also benevolent and peaceful. This subgenre includes *The Day the Earth Stood Still* (Robert Wise, 1951) and *This Island Earth* (Joseph Newman, 1954). Before 2001, this group consti-tuted the bulk of popular science fiction – the kind we love to make fun of today but which conveys a perennial charm: think of the remarkable *War of the Worlds* (Byron Haskin, 1953), based on H. G. Wells's novel. *2001* is indebted to this tradition, since the film is premised entirely on awaiting the revelation of the aliens (upon which a great iconographic tradition rests, especially thanks to comics and cover illustrations of sci-fi novels).

3. *The serial, with an evil genius* often sequestered in a hideout, with extra-ordinary weapons at his disposal, has been around since the silent era. From Fritz Lang's Dr Mabuse to the British James Bond series (whose great designer Ken Adam lent his support to *Dr Strangelove*), this is still a viable subgenre. It lent to *2001* a rich design tradition and several examples of hidden 'master-voices' or '*acousmêtres*', as I have described in *The Voice in Cinema*.

4. *Pacifist science fiction*: a prominent cycle during the years leading up to Kubrick's film, showing a world ravaged (or about to be) by nuclear war. Everyone knows Kubrick's amazing *Dr Strangelove* (1963), which ends in nuclear apocalypse. Popular memory has dimmed regarding such

interesting films as *On the Beach* (Stanley Kramer, 1959), about the death-throes of our earth as it slowly becomes covered by an atomic cloud; *The World, the Flesh and the Devil* (Ranald McDougall, 1959), which tells the story of several survivors in a New York devastated and depopulated by radiation; or *Panic in the Year Zero* (Ray Milland, 1962), and the excellent *Fail Safe* (Sidney Lumet, 1964), where Henry Fonda plays an American president desperately trying with his Russian counterpart to stop the machinery that has been set in motion to destroy the planet. This subgenre also lurks beneath the surface of *2001* in the way the film suggests the partitioning of the solar system (starting with the moon) by two powers who spy on each other. A film released in the same year as *2001*, *Ice Station Zebra* (John Sturges), with Rock Hudson, shows the two global powers in confrontation at the North Pole.

The moralising tendency that underlies most of these works is a staple of science-fiction movies. In *The Fly* (Kurt Neumann, 1958), *The Incredible Shrinking Man*, or in the Japanese *Godzilla* series directed by Inoshira Honda, the monsters are often products of imprudence and human folly. These films often end with a deistic, spiritualistic or humanistic profession of faith, which is part of the 'prophetic' and 'apocalyptic' tradition of the genre, also illustrated in films such as *The Day the Earth Stood Still* or *This Island Earth*, which were made as anti-nuclear warnings.

Based on a short story Clarke initially submitted to a Christmas story contest, *2001* is also dominated by the idea of waiting for a 'message', but a message that in this case is deliberately obscure and ambivalent.

5. *Totalitarian science fiction.* After the novels of George Orwell (whose *1984*, published in 1949, was brought to the screen twice – in 1956 by Michael Anderson, and in 1984 by Michael Radford) and Aldous Huxley (*Brave New World*, 1932) among others, but also of Franz Kafka, totalitarian science fiction depicts a future where Utopian ambitions become perverted, leading to a society of total regimentation, police surveillance and exploitation. I should also mention two French New Wave films in this tradition: François Truffaut's *Fahrenheit 451* (1966), based on a Ray Bradbury story, and especially Jean-Luc Godard's *Alphaville, A Strange Adventure of Lemmy Caution* (1965).

Auteur Science Fiction?

Situated in a future that is our present, but which the director invites us to imagine through the magic of words as being another world, Godard's *Alphaville* shows a computer named Alpha 60. Its close-up, 'placeless' voice (as harsh and grating as *2001*'s voice of Hal is smooth and gentle) sounds identical in every location of the action and set – just as Hal's does three years later in Kubrick's film. In *Alphaville*, which I imagine Kubrick saw as he was directing his own, the computer's eye is represented sometimes by a sort of headlight occupying the frame, and sometimes by a flashing light behind a wire mesh. But there are many differences too, and in some ways *2001* would invert the formula. In *Alphaville*, the image – in superb black-and-white shot by Raoul Coutard – shows us the urban world of the 60s, leaving it up to the dialogue and the narrator to transform the ordinary setting into the future ('Do you want to place a call outside the galaxy?' asks a phone operator). In *2001*, on the other hand, the image is what transports us into the future as the dialogue ('Did you have a pleasant flight?') might just as well be spoken in the 60s, avoiding science-fiction-speak at all costs. Any language of the 'Activate the hyper-energy generator' or 'We're entering the asteroid zone' type, the pride and joy of satirists, was carefully banished from the movie. Where *Alphaville* is a conjunction of pastiches – film noir meets popular science fiction (with Godardian themes grafted on) – Kubrick attempts to rethink the genre and jettison its verbal clichés.

The two films by Godard and Truffaut, and Chris Marker's masterpiece *La Jetée,* which is almost completely in stills, also remind us that science fiction intrigued several auteurs of the 60s before Kubrick. It haunted Antonioni and Fellini as well, though neither ever directed a science-fiction film *per se*. Antonioni, who later revealed his fondness for science fiction through the film-maker/protagonist of *Identification of a Woman* (1982), never took the plunge, but the modern world of his *Eclipse* (1962) and *Red Desert* (1964) is sometimes filmed to look like a futureworld. For example, the ending of *The Eclipse* consists of a non-narrative scene of silent images, which confers a cosmic dimension on nightfall over a modern city. In Fellini's *8½* (1963), Guido, Fellini's alter ego played by Marcello Mastroianni, is a director preparing a movie (the set has been built) but he never shoots it. The film-within-a-film is a science-fiction story about humans emigrating in a rocket after an atom bomb has destroyed the earth. And the 1969 *Satyricon*, a trip into the 'pagan' past of Rome, is the closest Fellini gets to his idea of science fiction.[5] Already in 1968 he had transposed Poe's *Toby Dammit* into a slightly futuristic world.

It should be kept in mind that the portrait I have drawn of pre-*2001* science fiction focuses exclusively on cinema. It was quite another story for literature, which for a long time – mainly in the United States but also in Eastern and Western Europe – had produced sophisticated and ambitious writers with fascinating themes. We might go so far as to say there were geniuses among them, such as Philip K. Dick, an author whom the cinema would discover, even pillage, only much later. One aspect of the evolution of the science-fiction film, particularly after *2001*, can be analysed as a major effort to 'catch up' by developing screenplays as complex and mature as literature had traditionally been.

A Decade of 'Op Art' Experimentation

Let us recall another long-lost source of *2001*'s inspiration: 60s cinema's taste for op art and pop art graphics. These tendencies are present in isolated scenes of numerous films of the time, science fiction or otherwise. Some examples are Louis Malle's *Zazie dans le métro* (1960 – perhaps Malle's best film, visually speaking), *The Nutty Professor* (Jerry Lewis, 1963 – the transformation sequences), *Le Bonheur* (Agnès Varda, 1965), *Persona* (Bergman, 1966), *Daisies* (Vera Chytilova, 1966), *Who Are You Polly Magoo?* (William Klein, France 1967), *Skidoo* (Otto Preminger, 1968), *Toby Dammit* (Federico Fellini, 1968), Blake Edwards's *The Party* (1968). Let us also include Clouzot's *La Prisonnière* (1968), and of course Godard's output of the 60s, notably *Pierrot le Fou* (1965) and *Made in USA* (1967), Jacques Tati, Federico Fellini (*Juliet of the Spirits*, 1965) and Richard Lester's *The Knack* (1965) and *Help!* (1965). This op/pop sensibility often arose from experimentation with new film stocks, as well as the fact that many of the European art directors were working in colour for the first time. Psychedelic culture inspired more than a few wild sequences – for instance, in a lesser-known Roger Corman film of 1967 (written by Jack Nicholson!) that was appropriately called *The Trip*.

The empty frame, futurism and desert(ed) landscapes permeate many films of the time. *2001* comes after Antonioni's *Red Desert* and is contemporaneous with other films where the idea of *rarefaction* is prominent. Consider the elements *2001* has in common with Tati's *Playtime*, for example: their plots have the same elliptical quality, the same sequential construction in blocs, the same focus on emptiness and distancing of affect.

In what may perhaps be an oversimplification but which also rings true, Jacques Goimard has written that '*2001* is the first film since Griffith's *Intolerance* [1917] to be both a superproduction and an experimental film.'[6] Let us also throw *Playtime* into this ring. In both cases, the director is putting a new spin on genres extremely familiar to the public, science fiction in one case and comedy in the other.

In 1968 it was not yet possible to perceive the similarity in these two films. *Playtime* was not seen very widely upon its release. Buoyed by an imminent moon mission, *2001* was one of the smash hits of 1968, a year of agitation by youth movements worldwide.

Kubrick's Career

The auteur theory is often contested in France today by people such as Noël Burch who were once its most fervent apologists. I have been actively occupied with reviving it for some time. Rather than throw the whole thing out, and reduce a film to a concatenation of individual chance factors, I prefer, as I wrote in my book on Lynch, to 'bring the *politique of auteurs* into a dialectical relationship with the *politique of the work*'.[7] In other words, the work must be considered in a *contradictory* relationship with its director and with the director's intention, of which it is far from being merely the obedient reflection.

Kubrick – who laboured mightily in order to be producer, co-writer and final arbiter of everything in his films – was famous for overseeing from his office in England the smallest details of their distribution, and he presents the reassuring portrait of the 'complete director'. Like others, however, he was operating in the real world, and like others he worked with collaborators, based on concrete conditions on the one hand and with his unconscious on the other. What ended up as *2001*, now that the dust has settled, is not necessarily a film over which Kubrick had complete control.

Kubrick was born on 26 July 1928 into a Bronx Jewish family of central European origin. His father was a doctor, and he grew up in an open-minded and cultivated environment. An average student more lacking in motivation than intelligence, he developed an interest in jazz – he played drums in a band – and also chess and photography. The latter skill helped to get him hired by *Look* magazine while still an adolescent; he went on to spend five years there as a reporter. This job gave him an intimate knowl-edge of photographic technique (on his films he was completely involved in the visual aspects, and operated the camera himself when possible). These years also imbued in him a passion for reality: the documentarist's vision remains very much in evidence in his fictional works. We can see this tendency in his use of certain modes of presenting events (titles, third-person voice-over narrations), and his concern for precision, often mis-taken for coldness. We should also note that certain subjects in his photos or photo sequences resurface in the films: the boxing match, and the irony of the zoo where people watch monkeys and monkeys watch people.

Kubrick was a cinephile. He greatly admired Akira Kurosawa and Max Ophuls, whose *Madame de ...* would remain one of his favourite works. In 1950, he made two documentary shorts that he wrote, filmed, sound-recorded and edited himself: *Day of the Fight*, a day in the life of a boxer (the boxer recurs in several of his films), and *Flying Padre*, about a priest in New Mexico who travels to his parishioners in a small airplane. These two works, and an 'industrial', *The Seafarers* (1953), have a voice-over nar-rator, a classic technique of the documentary, and which he would extend to fictional works like *The Killing* and *Barry Lyndon*. But a more general penchant for documentary-style fiction can also be seen in 'neo-realist' American crime films of the late 40s and early 50s, notably those produced by Mark Hellinger (*The Naked City*, Jules Dassin, 1948) and Louis de Rochemont (*Boomerang*, Elia Kazan, 1947). Kubrick thus began film-making as a participant in a realist current that flourished after the war, whose best-known expression was the Italian school but which was just about everywhere.[8]

His first features – *Fear and Desire* (1953, a war drama focused on a small group of characters) and *Killer's Kiss* (1955, a thriller), both financed by loans and modest revenues, were low-budget exercises that had no great commercial success but allowed Kubrick to immerse himself in all aspects of film from shooting to editing and post-synchronisation. His visual style is already clearly evident in the sharp contrast and definition to the black-and-white imagery, as is his pessimistic world view. These two projects led to a fruitful long-term collaboration with the producer James B. Harris (born in 1928), who would himself later direct such interesting films as *Some Call it Loving* (1973) and *Cop* (1987, based on James Ellroy).

The first two results of Harris–Kubrick Pictures were *The Killing* (1956), based on Lionel White's novel *Clean Break* – an achronologically told story about a botched holdup, with Sterling Hayden – and *Paths of Glory* (1957), in which French army officers order executions of soldiers 'to set an example' during the First World War. The latter film, both moving and acerbic, stars Kirk Douglas, and brought Kubrick into the limelight as a gifted young film-maker. While not officially banned in France, *Paths of Glory* had to wait years to be shown there.

As the producer and star of the progressive epic *Spartacus* (1960), Kirk Douglas appealed to Kubrick as a replacement for Anthony Mann at short notice. The work, written by Dalton Trumbo and whose screenplay Kubrick would repudiate, nevertheless familiarised him with the difficulties of big-budget productions. (Before *Spartacus*, he was approached to direct *One-Eyed Jacks*, with Marlon Brando, who eventually ended up directing the Western himself.) The Kubrick–Harris collaboration continued with a project that was a long time in the making, *Lolita* (1962), adapting Nabokov's novel; Nabokov wrote the screenplay, but Kubrick reworked it as well.[9] For economic reasons among others, a portion of the film, whose subject obviously scandalised many in the United States, was filmed in England, where Kubrick later chose to settle for good. Although he once held a pilot's licence, he acquired a phobia of airplane trips and apparently of any high-speed travel, even cars, as a result of an incident that almost cost him his life. After the mid-60s he lived within a small perimeter that he rarely left. He would scout locations in the environs of London for his films, whether the stories were set in the United States, Vietnam or . . . in outer space. In certain cases where he really needed other settings for an exterior, he would send second units out into the world to shoot them.

It was in the 60s that Kubrick created and obtained the unique status of director/star that he enjoyed until his death. He was now dealing with big studios like MGM and Warner, who arranged special contracts for him as producer, assuring his total control over his films.

Extremes and Contrasts

In hindsight, *2001*, the second superproduction by Kubrick, can be seen as the middle instalment of a 'science-fiction' trilogy, between *Dr Strangelove* (1963)[10] and *A Clockwork Orange* (1971). Both of these are in a much more burlesque mode. *Strangelove* (on the nuclear threat) and *2001* manifest not only the immoderate ambition to consider the fate of the planet and the human species, but also feature the theme of the perfect system that goes haywire. *2001* and *A Clockwork Orange* also constitute a couple, the latter signalling the triumphant return of what *2001* represses in its human characters: sexuality, violence, the desire for power. *A Clockwork Orange* is even a critique of *2001* in soliciting us to be wary of music as a symbol of the life force.

Kubrick has often been described as a director who loved to take on all genres – epics (*Spartacus*), film noir (*Killer's Kiss*, *The Killing*), period film (*Barry Lyndon*), horror film (*The Shining*) and war film (*Fear and Desire*, *Paths of Glory*, *Full Metal Jacket*) – with the intention of 'subverting' or undercutting them. This perspective seems reductive to me. A true artist has other things to do than childishly parade himself as someone who 'doesn't do things like other people'. Besides, the different genres in which Kubrick worked already had a rich and variegated history; there existed no monolithic structure to be 'undercut'. It is also easy to show that the theme of war explicitly or implicitly runs through much of his work, in both the films he completed and in the big project he began after *2001* that never came to fruition, a life of Napoleon. Outside the 'official' war films noted above, battle scenes occur in *Spartacus* and *Barry Lyndon*, and plot situations involving hunting and predation can be found in almost all the features.

What we can say with confidence, however, is that Kubrick loved to take a genre at a certain stage in its evolution, learn from its past successes and failures, and bring something new to it – not necessarily to take a counter-stance, but also not to rest content with passing on conventional formulas. The genre film, via the multiplicity of references that it brings to the viewer's mind and via the expectations it sets up of a certain body of rules, lends itself well to formal experimentation. From the outset, like Sergio Leone with his Westerns, Kubrick loved to *call attention to form* in his films, through his idiosyncratic choices in narration and *mise en scène* and through dividing films into episodes and acts. Several of the films play on the idea of symmetry or dissymmetry: a film may show the rise and fall of a person's fate or a system (*The Killing, Lolita, Barry Lyndon, A Clockwork Orange*); between segments there can be a marked change of tone, era or style (*2001, A Clockwork Orange, Full Metal Jacket*); or one film can be the counterbalance to its predecessor (for example, the optimism and seriousness of *2001* contrasts with the pessimistic and farcical tone of *Dr Strangelove*).

On the other hand, Kubrick's films demonstrate great consistency in visual choices. In most of the films he had a predilection for wide-angle lenses (which dilate and expand space and exaggerate perspective) and for great depth of field, as well as for an extremely sharp and detailed, often contrasty, image. It is a visual style that emphasises the sensory shock inherent in each cut between shots; each cut feels like a decision, a choice, a chess move.

Kubrick's oeuvre manifests striking unity, as Michel Ciment pointed out in his analysis of the scene types that recur through the films. This unity also sometimes resides in strong contrasts between one work and the next. We might call Kubrick an extremist, though this is not meant pejoratively: an extremist both in the aesthetic stances taken on each film, and in the way he constantly reinvented himself as a film-maker.

The commercial success of *2001* and its status as a classic make us forget that it is a daring film of enormous contrasts. From the bellowing aggressivity of the apes in the first part, for example, the film moves to the smooth professionalism of the astronauts. The same goes for visual style: for example, in opposition to cuts and static shots in some sequences, there is slow drifting and floating in others, and the continuous metamorphoses

of the 'psychedelic' episode. The fixed camera and rigid frame of numerous shots contrast with the hand-held and unstable camera elsewhere.

The 'extreme' is a notion that has become banal in ordinary discourse
(certainly in advertising), but it is rarely truly engaged and pushed to its
limits. Kubrick deals in extremes from film to film, as if they are opposite
sides of one and the same world. Take just the directing of actors: whereas
in the two overacted films *Dr Strangelove* and *A Clockwork Orange* the
director pushed his actors to externalise everything, *2001* attempts the
other extreme, a smooth, clean, restrained, almost invisible style, to the
point where we have difficulty remembering that this film required of its
actors utmost concentration and creativity.

Another kind of extreme contrast emerges on the level of screenwriting
style. Twelve years later, *The Shining* was worlds apart from *2001* in its
hyperexplicitness. Everything we need to know about the word 'shining',
about the madness that stalks Jack Torrance, and about the murder in the
haunted room, is told to us in the first few minutes. Furthermore, it is
almost hilariously overplayed by the hysterical pair of Jack Nicholson and
Shelley Duvall. Thus a film that explains everything ends up feeling as
impenetrable as a film that explains nothing. Both present a surface with
no fissures, unassailably mysterious.

A Ruthless Perfectionism

Kubrick's genius springs not only from his strong personality, possessed of
driving personal obsessions, but also from his basic intellectual and artistic honesty. This honesty guaranteed that he never compromised his
intentions and his demands, nor the quality of execution he was driven to
bestow on his work (for Kubrick, technique was not a 'plus', but an integral part of his ruthless perfectionism).[11]

Kubrick exercised enormous care in directing his films: this is immediately visible, as in a well-kept household, through the clean camerawork,
the precision of the acting, the hallucinatory clarity of the image and sound,
and the often impeccable symmetry of framing. This obsessive care mirrors the care the fictional characters themselves devote to accomplish their
task or their project, like parents anxious to satisfy immediately the slightest need. Many of the films' heroes are filled to bursting for their

immediate satisfaction, and we cannot see from where any waiting or desire might sneak in. The Overlook Hotel of *The Shining*, with its stocks of food to last for years, the Orion or the Discovery in *2001,* where everything arrives when it is ordered, the apartment of Alex's parents where he still lives in *A Clockwork Orange*, the manor house where Barry Lyndon's pampered child lives are familial cocoons that are both 'perfect' and oppressive.

The particular way Kubrick had of responding during interviews – appealing to logic in order to discuss questions that were put to him – reminds us that his films were made by rationally considering various possibilities while at the same time showing the inadequacy of this method. Hence his fascination for domains where logic and calculus are supposed to prevail, but easily lead to absurdity – such as the military, which Kubrick, like Tolstoy, observed with insight, particularly in *Paths of Glory* and *Full Metal Jacket*.

Aside from *Spartacus* perhaps (but this is a film Kubrick did not see as personally his), Kubrick critiques heroism. In *2001*, although Dave Bowman takes some risks and faces some difficult choices, he is the very opposite of a superman, and everything in the directing takes great pains to 'de-heroise' the action scenes. When Dave disconnects Hal, for example, there is no emphasis on the real risks he might be facing.

Kubrick loved telling stories about systems that go out of kilter. *The Killing* depicts the meticulous planning of a big robbery that ends in failure because of an unforeseen detail. In *Barry Lyndon*, the rise of Redmond Barry would seem to be inevitable in this story of a surname that becomes a given name.[12] In *The Shining*, the conditions are perfect to allow Jack Torrance to work on his novel: plenty of time, peace and quiet, a devoted wife and an obedient son. And in *Full Metal Jacket*, the training regimen for marines is presented as impeccable, the exception being a difficult recruit's plunge into madness.

Michel Ciment put it well: the Kubrickian film is shot through with slips and undoings. The foregrounding of the structure of the film, the clarity of its image, all seem designed to highlight all the more the *lapsus* when it occurs while leaving open the question of the place of the misstep.

But most of all, completely banally and stupidly, one might say, Kubrick was an observer fascinated by human beings and the traps they set for themselves, a more sympathetic observer than he is usually given credit for being. His irony is by no means a sardonic distance. The very act of making films about human destiny that are so finely worked, so demanding and impassioned, is an act of love, faith and compassion.

All the foregoing is the portrait that could be made of Kubrick before *Eyes Wide Shut*. Released after the director's death in 1999, *Eyes Wide Shut* surprised everyone and opened new perspectives. It stands apart in Kubrick's oeuvre, yet at the same time, it seems to me that it answers to *2001*, as I shall argue in the final chapter.

Notes

1   According to Arthur C. Clarke (*2001: The Final Odyssey*), the US's descent into the Vietnam War, and then the Watergate scandal, aided in dampening public interest in the 'conquest' of space and giving it a low governmental priority.

2   This important interview is reprinted in Schwam, pp. 272–300.

3   It is not surprising that three British films show up on my quickly assembled A-list. England has long been a Mecca of fantasy and science-fiction films, as well as the visual-effects serial (James Bond, for example), and has nurtured the development of great technicians and designers of special effects – one of the factors that encouraged Kubrick to shoot *2001* in London.

4   These can be found by the 40s, with novels like *Renaissance* (Raymond F. Jones, 1944) and *The World of non-A* (A. E. van Vogt, 1945), and then *Solar Lottery* (Philip K. Dick, 1955) and many others.

5   One can even see science-fiction elements in the modern Rome that is depicted in *Ginger and Fred* (1985).

6   Goimard, 'Une Odyssée formelle', *L'Avant-Scène*, nos. 231/2, 1979.

7   [*Politique* does not mean politics here, but 'policy', or critical approach in this case. Chion argues for bringing auteur criticism into a dialectical relationship with formal (textual) criticism. – Translator.]

8   For example, in a Mizoguchi film such as *Women of the Night* (1948).

9   Harris–Kubrick had bought the rights to the book in proof, before it was published – and thus before its immense *succès de scandale*, which surely

would have skyrocketed the property's price beyond what they could have afforded. According to Harris, Nabokov's screenplay was rewritten in detail by the director and himself.

10 *Dr Strangelove* was an example of what was called speculative fiction, a genre that imagined the consequences of an atomic war or some other present-day catastrophe.

11 In my opinion the cinema is too often considered solely as an art of conception, and not often enough as an art of execution. The import of execution is not limited to acting (itself underexamined in film studies), but also includes such things as musical 'interpretation', camera movement and lighting effects by those who make these things happen: orchestra musicians, camera operators, lighting technicians.

12 Joining the nobility by marriage to the widow Lady Lyndon, Redmond Barry adopts the name Barry Lyndon, the name of the husband he defied in the past. He would henceforth be considered an interloper, especially by Lord Bullingdon, the son from the first marriage.

Chapter Three
Structure

2001 as it Actually Is

You are in a cinema, and you see *2001* for the first or second time. What do you see, and what do you hear? It is certainly not the same experience today as it was when the film hit movie screens for the first time.

In recounting the movie's plot, people have a tendency to rely on sources other than the film itself. First and foremost, there is Arthur C. Clarke's novel (his personal variation on the original screenplay, on which he collaborated with Kubrick), published after the film's release. Plot summaries from press releases are also called upon, as well as some other standard studies and texts.

If we wish to recount the plot of *2001* based solely on our viewing – what I shall try to do here – we must forget about these external sources. Then certain things turn out not to be clear, and it becomes more difficult to draw connections.

For example, in the summaries and commentaries, the dominant anthropoid ape is often dubbed Moonwatcher, because that is his name in the novel. The film never names him either in dialogue (for good reason!) or in titles or closing credits. There is also the issue of a 'neurosis' in Hal, caused by the contradiction between his knowledge of the real goal of the Jupiter mission (find evidence of extraterrestrial life), which he must hide from the crew, and his role of serving the crew. The film tells us nothing about this either, only that Hal *knew* and Dave and Frank *did not know*.

People also take as a given that the bedroom suite in Regency style where Dave lands at the end, and where we watch him age, is a sort of zoo cage made for him from pictures of human life that the aliens have picked up, so that he may live and be observed there without feeling homesick. But the film shows no aliens, nor does it indicate that this room is an observation chamber. The sole indication of any possibly living presence is the chaotic reverberant noise that surrounds the room for a while – suggesting that the space outside the room is perennially filled with this din – and also the final reappearance of the monolith before the aged Dave. You can say nothing more. It seems to me that any analysis of *2001* must respect its lacunary, indeterminate quality, and any interpreting you do must be accompanied with reservations. If you wish to interpret, you need to start from the literal text of the film itself.

So let us try to tell the film story that the screen actually presents to us.

After the title '2001: A Space Odyssey', and a prologue showing celestial bodies in alignment, accompanied by a triumphal music cue, a second title appears: 'The Dawn of Man'.

In a desolate landscape, we see a small clan of apes headed by a chief; their vocalisation is limited to grunting. They feed on meagre vegetation in the company of peaceful tapirs who are eating the same things. They fear attack by predators such as tigers. They defend their territory – a small watering hole – against another clan of the same species.[1]

One morning, the first ape to awaken notices a black vertical slab, perfectly smooth and perpendicular, near their dwelling. He alerts his fellow creatures, and they gather around the object, to the accompaniment of a choral music cue. Soon after, as he is picking among some tapir bones, we see the leader pick up a long bone and make use of it as an instrument to shatter the animal's skeleton and skull. The editing suggests – by means of inserted shots of the monolith and of a tapir collapsing, and the sound of the triumphal music from the opening – that from now on he will use the bone as a weapon to destroy his prey.

Later we see the same tribe eating meat; they have become carnivorous. The monolith is no longer where it had appeared.

In a battle with another clan of apes, the clan leader – the one who had the bone revelation – uses the bone to strike an enemy ape, and his companions follow suit. In a gesture of triumph, after the victory, he throws the bone skywards.

This bone, turning over and over in slow motion in the diurnal sky, is suddenly replaced by an elongated spacecraft moving through the interplanetary night. From this image the film segues to a series of shots of objects in space revolving around the earth and moon. One of them, shaped like an arrow, moves towards a wheel-shaped orbiting space station.[2]

We are given to understand that the time now is 2001, although the date is mentioned only in the film's title and never comes up in the dialogue or image.

A man disembarks at the station. This is the American Heywood Floyd, later identified as the president of the National Council of Astronautics. During his stopover, in the lobby of a Hilton hotel in space, he has an interview with a Russian scientist who asks him about an American moon base that has gone mysteriously silent, and about which rumours of an epidemic are circulating. Without entirely denying the rumour, Floyd cites his obligation not to divulge sensitive information. We understand from the discussion between Floyd and the Russians that there is also a Soviet base on the moon.

Floyd goes to the moon. In the underground base of Clavius, in the course of a meeting, he reveals to us that the epidemic rumour is a diversion, a temporary ruse whose purpose is to hide a momentous discovery. Later, we learn what it is: an object has been unearthed that was 'deliberately buried' at a site on the moon four million years ago, and which emits a very strong magnetic field. Floyd travels to the site with other scientists, and we see a monolith similar in form and size to the one seen in the episode of the prehistoric apemen. When one of the astronauts tries to take a picture of his companions grouped in front of the object, the monolith emits a strident signal, just at the moment when the sun hits it (it is the lunar dawn).

Title: 'Jupiter Mission: 18 Months Later'.

The spaceship Discovery has been travelling for three weeks towards Jupiter on a long mission. On board are Dave Bowman, the head of the expedition, his assistant Frank Poole and three astronauts hibernating in individual white chilled compartments, scheduled to be awakened when the expedition nears its goal. The sixth passenger is a computer, a perfected specimen of the series HAL 9000, who speaks in a synthesised male voice that is suave and refined, and who sees through red 'eyes' installed throughout the ship. Hal controls all activity on the Discovery, and sees to the comfort of the passengers (both awake and hibernating).

Hal asks Dave how he feels about 'some extremely odd things about this mission' (why were three of the astronauts put to sleep just before take-off, after four months of training?), but Dave does not answer. Then Hal notifies him that a unit of the ship's antenna is about to fail. Dave jets out into space in a small spherical shuttle called a pod. He then goes out into the void in his space suit, manoeuvring with jets on his backpack; he removes the part from the antenna, replaces it with a new one and brings the suspect part back into the mother ship. Frank and Dave check the unit and find no defect; their conclusion is confirmed by a counter-check made back on earth at Mission Control. Hal appears to have made an error, but he denies this and attributes the mistake to humans. Dave and Frank climb into a pod for privacy and cut audio contact with Hal; they discuss possibly disconnecting the computer if they confirm that it is malfunctioning. Unfortunately, as we later discover, they do not realise that Hal can read their lips through a porthole.

Up to this point, the film has proceeded at a peaceful, neutral rhythm that might be called objective.

Suddenly, during Frank's turn to spacewalk into the void to reinstall the antenna unit, we see his pod attack him and cut off the airflow to his spacesuit. He dies. Dave goes out in a different pod to retrieve Frank's body as it turns over and over in the darkness. In his haste he neglects to put on his helmet. Hal – whom we realise has caused Frank's death by remote control – terminates the support systems for the three hibernating astronauts, who meet their demise in deathly silence.[3] When Dave tries to re-enter the Discovery, Hal, with whom he is communicating by radio, refuses him entry in the name of the higher interest of the mission; Hal also reveals his awareness of Dave's intention to disconnect him. At great peril, Dave manages to gain access into the Discovery, briefly passing through the vacuum of space, into an emergency airlock. He goes to Hal's memory centre, which we had not seen until now, and manually disconnects the computer in spite of Hal's pleas. Once Hal 'dies', a prerecorded message (made before the ship left on its mission, and designed to play when the ship neared Jupiter) reveals to Dave the real purpose of the voyage:[4] the discovery on the moon of a black monolith that is sending signals towards Jupiter, an object that has remained inert and whose function is a mystery.

This is the first 'action' sequence of *2001* in the classic sense, but it is narrated with hardly more drama than anything before or after.

A new title presents the next segment: 'Jupiter and Beyond the Infinite'.

From this point on, the film becomes much more of a 'sensory experience'.

Near Jupiter and its moons floating in space, we see the reappearance of a monolith like the previous one, but 'horizontal';[5] its size is impossible to gauge. It seems to welcome and guide Dave who is carried along in his spherical pod on a stellar trip. Through his eyes we are subjected to dizzying perspectives; we see galaxies, novas, cosmic and organic phenomena of indeterminate scale; we fly over grandiose landscapes in magical colours. Suddenly the trip is over; the pod and Dave inside, in his spacesuit, are now in the middle of what looks like a luxury hotel suite decorated in Regency style; it is comfortable and hermetically enclosed, but surrounded by some sort of cosmic noise.

Through a striking series of eyeline matches, we think three times that another person is present, but each time it is Dave, markedly older, in this space where he lives, eats and ages, apparently without ever having a single living contact. Finally he lies as a very old man on the bed, about to die, when the monolith appears, standing at the foot of the bed, and he stretches his hand out toward it. A large, glowing foetus takes his place on the bed.

While we hear the same triumphal music that had accompanied the ape's discovery of the 'tool', this perfectly formed male foetus with its eyes open, itself as huge as a planet and resembling a baby Dave, approaches the planet earth and slowly turns its eyes toward us ...

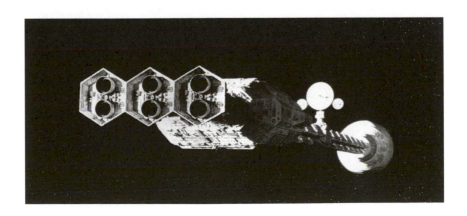

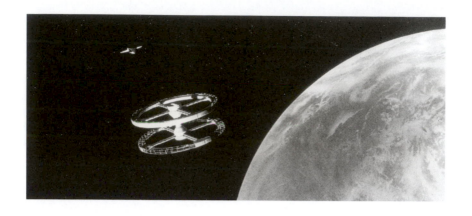

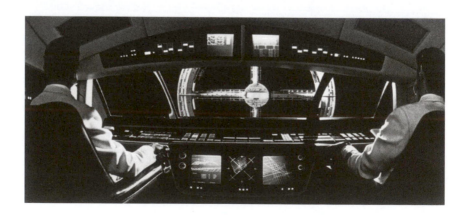

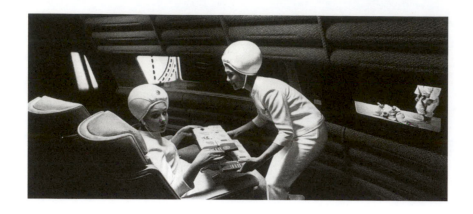

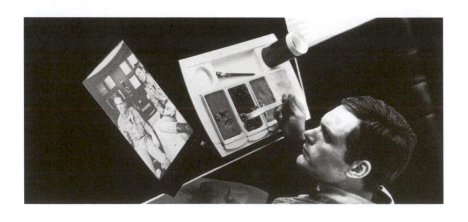

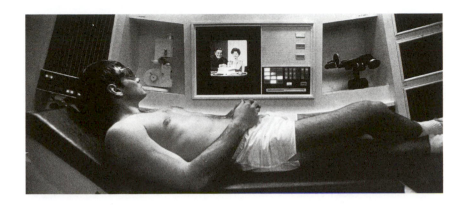

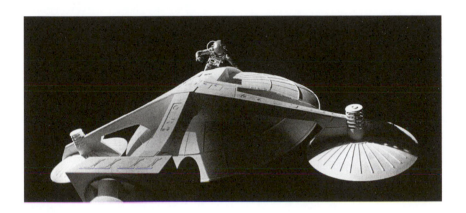

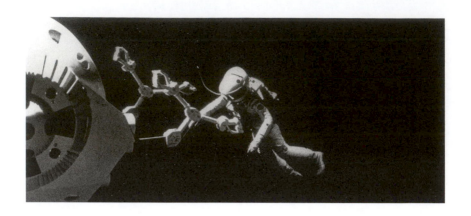

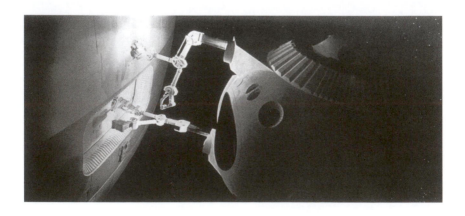

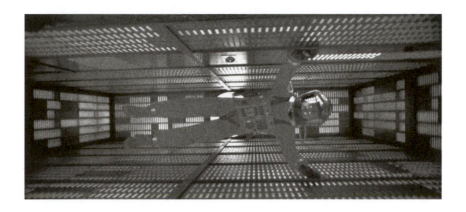

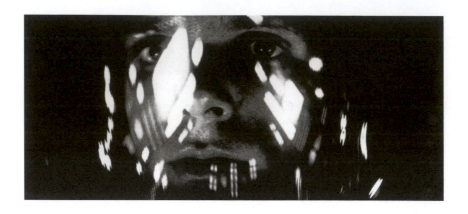

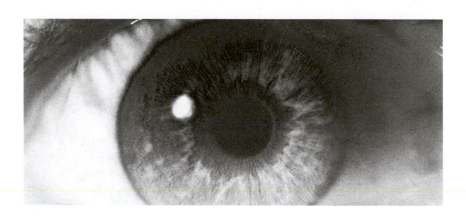

'The End', to the sound of Strauss's 'Blue Danube' Waltz.

The spectator leaving the cinema does not have the sense of having seen a finished, resolved, gap-free film. S/he has the impression that the film could go on, with more developments, other parts.

This impression is not created solely by the enigmatic character of certain story events, but also by the spectator's constant awareness of *form*, a form both strongly foregrounded and replete with rifts and absences. It is a form that consists of detached parts, and is a major aspect of the originality of *2001*.

Segmentation on Display

The question of whether and how a film is divided into parts, and whether and how the segmentation is marked, lies at the heart of film narrative. A narration or representation does not at all have the same meaning if it makes a display of its divisions – in acts, scenes, tableaux, songs, tunes, entrances, book chapters, comic strips, and so on, as is the case with almost all genres in existence before film[6] – or if it covers them up. In fact, the cinema is perhaps the first major popular narrative–representational genre in history that, at one stage of its evolution (the classical sound film), worked to completely hide its divisions, and avoided marking them consciously for the audience, thereby changing the rules of the game.[7]

As a rule, the silent film tended to foreground its segmentation, in sequences and/or acts, via a set of practices that included intertitles, the use of monochrome tints that differed according to the type of scene, musical accompaniment by individual numbers strung together, and so on – while the sound film tended to hide them. During the 60s, two directors contributed to marking the division of films into parts and scenes, in an attempt to deal with form 'out in the open'. One was Sergio Leone, whose Westerns were like Verdi operas. The other, with *2001*, was Stanley Kubrick. Only in the 80s and especially the 90s did the foregrounding of a film's structure, particularly through play with titles, become almost commonplace in popular cinema as well as in 'auteur' films.[8]

The problem of the construction of *2001* in two, three, four or n parts is not just a minor one, since it orders our understanding of the film and the effects it produces. More than any of Kubrick's previous or subsequent films, this film announces its divisions in every way possible: with titles, with an almost totally new crop of characters in each section, with an intermission accompanied by music (Ligeti's *Atmosphères*) in the film's original release, and with pieces of music deployed in wide swaths, which succeed in cutting the film into very recognisable chunks (for example, the 'Blue Danube' Waltz begins with the first vision of the future and ends on the spaceship's arrival at the station).

But what is important is that the points where the different division markers occur do not always coincide. This non-coincidence among the breaks, depending on which segmentation criteria you choose, gives the film a stimulant effect. We are obliged to choose what makes sense and how it makes sense. This non-coinciding makes the viewer actively compare, find symmetries, be on the lookout for 'rhymes'.

Two, Three or Four Parts?

If you go by the intermission that was part of the original version, *2001* is a *two-part* film. When you work on *2001* from a video copy, or from the film projected in a modern cinema, you tend to forget that originally the film, which was longer than average, once had an intermission. The spell of the story was maintained with Ligeti's *Atmosphères* piped throughout the auditorium and foyer; the music was actually recorded on to the magnetic strip of the 70mm film and played from the projector.

This intermission, no longer practised today,[9] maintained suspense by interrupting the film in the middle of the most 'dramatic' episode, and at a point particularly pregnant with questions about its characters, dialogue, and conflicts: what does Hal 'think' about what he is 'seeing' through the pod porthole? Is he going to be unplugged? More specifically, the break comes right after the shot of the silent mouths of Poole and Bowman, seen in a subjective shot through Hal's eye. We are watching both an illustration and an inversion of the *acousmêtre*.[10] Hal is a voice without a mouth, through whose eye we see mouths without voices.

One critic came up with this amusing theory:

> Much of the critical hostility to *Space Odyssey* originated in the theater lobby during intermission. Critics (some of whom seemed to dislike movies and

wish they were more like books) met their friends and found that nobody was able to verbalize what the film, so far, had 'meant'.[11]

If you go by the section titles only, *2001* is in *three* parts. According to this scheme, the first part includes both the apemen and Floyd. There is something idiotic about this, for the most striking division of *2001* occurs where no title is shown to mark it, in the elliptical cut from the bone to the spacecraft. But it is here that the segmentation exercise becomes meaningful: if there *weren't* those deliberately pompous introductory phrases – 'The Dawn of Man', 'Jupiter Mission', 'Jupiter and Beyond the Infinite' – the absence of a title at the exact moment of that dramatic cut would not have the power that it does have to transport us. It is entirely because of those words that this cut, this absence, becomes the unstated and unmarked division upon which the entire film is constructed. There is no unsaid except in the space of the said.

If we calculate according to the film's temporal ellipses, we also have three blocks, since there are only two jumps in time. The first is a hiatus of several million years, the other is a year and a half – apart from the fact that, in the last sequences of the cosmic trip and the room, time gets diluted and lost. So there too, the specific designation of 'eighteen months later' prepares us for something further on, when Dave is carried 'beyond the infinite', the loss of temporal scale and the blurring of different ages in one and the same character. Again, the said creating the unsaid.

Finally, if we take narrative segmentation as our principal criterion, which is the one most frequently invoked by critics, we have *four* parts: the apes and the monolith; Heywood Floyd's mission; the Discovery mission eighteen months later; and Bowman's trip 'beyond the infinite' (with the understanding that Bowman is the only character to appear in more than one section).

We could also segment the film according to any number of other criteria: appearances of the monolith, statements of specific musical pieces (no one piece appears in all of the film's time periods), the relation between dialogue scenes and those with no dialogue, sequences with and without titles. And all these segmentation schemes underscore what they cannot contain and name. All the precise details supplied in *2001* create imprecision; all its plenitude creates voids, stimulating the play of rhymes, repetitions, parallels, echoes.

Here I shall adopt the division into four parts (see the table on page 61), framed by two brief supplementary and symmetrical sections. At the beginning, behind the brief opening titles, there is the alignment of celestial bodies, and at the end the confrontation between planet earth and the Star Child. The symmetry between the introduction and the coda is reinforced by the use of the same music from *Thus Spake Zarathustra*.

'The Dawn of Man' has all the earmarks of a classical prologue, in the false-etymological sense sometimes given to this term (that which precedes the word)[12] since it shows a species of evolved apes deprived of speech.

The next sequence is at once one of the visual highlights of the film, and an intentionally long, dragging prologue for the section that follows it. It alternates two types of scenes: a sort of visual amusement park in slow motion to the symphonic accents of the 'Blue Danube' Waltz, and dialogue scenes that are extremely static, as Kubrick is sometimes inclined towards. The character Heywood Floyd is the main thread weaving through this part, present in every scene.

The third section, which revolves around the voyage of the Discovery, is the longest, at fifty-seven minutes, and the closest in spirit to the classical cinema, which by no means detracts from its originality. It has characters, conflicts, suspense, a 'rebellion', an ordeal, and so on. This long section in turn functions retroactively like a long prologue to what follows.

The fourth, entitled 'Jupiter and Beyond the Infinite', is the first to retain a character from a previous part, but he utters not a word, nor does he act in a way that affects the plot. His fate totally taken in hand, Dave Bowman figures only as a captive representative of the human species, and as an open eye.

The brief image of the 'astral foetus' (I call it thus with reference to the essay by Jean-Paul Dumont and Jean Monod) or the Star Child, as the original screenplay calls it, can well be considered in turn like ... an overture.

In fact, with *2001*, each part is subtended by the idea of an *after* and ends with a beginning: the beginning of man, the awakening of the monolith on the moon, the revelation to Dave of the monolith and therefore another species besides man, the possible beginning of a new species of superman.

I have spoken of the general form, but we must not ignore the story rhythm and the film's tone, at once both familiar and epic. On this point let me propose a parallel with a Russian writer whose name may perhaps surprise the reader.

A Cinema of Discontinuum

To approach the question of narrative and form in Kubrick, we might learn from the example of Tolstoy. André Gide wrote in his journal about *War and Peace* that, in the process of providing descriptions to the minutest details, Tolstoy lined up his chapters like so many static dioramas, dioramas lacking in the art of the significant detail, of cause and effect, of perspective. This criticism has more to it than other more adulatory assessments. Tolstoy's flattening, with neither perspective nor chiaroscuro, of a dense reality on to a surface crowded with details, arises from a certain philosophy of history, of war and determinism. The author clearly articulates this philosophy in a little-read essay that constitutes the end of his novel. For him, the *ridiculous character* is the one who convinces himself that he has control over the course of events – the Emperor Napoleon in person, or in any case Napoleon as the writer makes him move and act; while the *positive character*, embodied by General Kutuzov, is the one who understands the illusion that produces this pretence and who, letting himself be carried by the course of things with apparent fatalism, reaches a mastery of another order.

Here are three points in common between Tolstoy and Kubrick, who are otherwise so different: their common interest in Napoleon, and more generally in war and illusions of strategy; their critique of voluntarism (that is, the belief that if you do something as well as you can, it will produce the desired result); and last, on the level of style, the cold, hard light they love to cast on all they depict.

The strong differences between them emerge on the level of form. While Tolstoy approaches the novel as an infinitely extensible framework, Kubrick manipulates this equalisation of details for a formal effect linked to the rhythm and tempo of cinema. For Kubrick, the 'by the menu' quality of certain parts emphasises all the more pointedly the violence of any ruptures or wrenchings that occur during the implacable course of the film.

And while a novel can be read, leafed through or devoured altogether in whatever rhythms its reader decides on, in the cinema it is the director who turns the pages at the speed *he* chooses. Kubrick's cinema, with its very calculated tempo and its cruel editing, as if cut by a razor, turns those pages with an authority that cannot be argued with. This 'turning', especially in many passages of *2001*, is the shot transitions.

It is difficult to make these edits feel any more 'imposed' in a film than they are in *2001*, just as it is difficult to highlight as much as Kubrick does the impression that a film is a stitched-together juxtaposition of scenes in succession. And on the vertical axis,[13] the superimposing of music on to images in *2001* can seem forced, rigid and graceless, but you have to either take it or leave it. Not because the music is all drawn from pre-existing concert works (Bernard Eisenschitz remarked that this practice is as old as cinema itself), but rather because of the way the superimposing is done. The music is *exhibited*, and is rarely mixed with sound effects, more rarely still with dialogue; it refuses to melt in or make common cause with other soundtrack elements.

Section	Music	Dialogue
Opening credits 2′	*Zarathustra*	no
A. The Dawn of Man: 14′	no	cries
	Requiem (A2)	no
	no	cries
	Zarathustra (A3)	no
B. (no title): 33′		
Voyage to space station	'Blue Danube' Waltz (B1)	no
At the station	no	yes
Voyage to the moon	'Blue Danube' (B3)	pronounced, not heard
Floyd's speech	no	yes
To the monolith	*Lux aeterna* (B5)	no
	no	yes
	Lux aeterna (B5)	no
The visit to the monolith	*Requiem*	no

C. Jupiter Mission 18 months later: 57′
31′15″; Intermission; 25′45″

Exposition	*Gayaneh* (C1)	no
	no	yes
	Gayaneh (C3)	yes
The drama I		yes
INTERMISSION	*Atmosphères*	
The drama II	no	yes

D. Jupiter and Beyond the Infinite: 22′25″

Cosmic trip	*Requiem* (D1), *Atmosphères* (D2–4)	no
The bedroom	no	
	Zarathustra (D7)	no
End	*Zarathustra* (D8)	
End credits 3′53″	'Blue Danube'	

In sum, Kubrick does everything possible to render the film a *discontinuum* – in the image of the famous black monolith, whose obtuse and irrefutable presence causes rupture in the scenes where it enters, for it never integrates into its environment – neither with the natural animal setting at the beginning, nor with the human setting of the central episode, nor finally with the cosmic universe of the end.

The monolith and the structure of the film are thus intimately related.

Notes

1   The viewer is not supposed to know that these images are supposedly emblematic of an epoch of drought on earth that put the existence of the apes in jeopardy; this is what the voice-over commentary, which was ultimately omitted, was to explain. It might give the apes a specificity: *these* apes live by a small pond. The same goes for the sparseness of the vegetation.

2 The shots of the large wheel being approached by the arrowlike spacecraft, called Orion in the screenplay, clearly suggest sexual penetration.

3 Hal's 'responsibility' can be deduced only from a succession of dire warnings flashing on control monitors (see below).

4 In the novel, it is clearly established that the three astronauts in hibernation were put in that state because, unlike Dave and Frank, they knew the secret mission. In the film, nothing gives us this information and a sentence in the speech recorded by Floyd even seems to contradict this thesis.

5 Horizontal obviously in relation to the film frame; we are, after all, in space.

6 Even if Wagner abolished divisions of his operas into choruses, arias and so on, he retained and even emphasised the division by acts, going so far as to specify by what manner the curtain must fall at the end of each, and what music to play at the end of the intermissions to bring the audience back into the auditorium.

7 Fade-outs are almost always calculated to be perceived subliminally, so the audience does not have time to realise that the film is moving to another segment.

8 To cite only films of the 90s: David Fincher's *Seven* (1995), with titles indicating the passing days; Lars von Trier's 1996 *Breaking the Waves*, which has chapter headings; Wayne Wang's *Smoke* (1995, written by Paul Auster); and the works of Pascale Ferran including *Petits arrangements avec les morts* (1994) and Arnaud Desplechin's *Comment je me suis disputé ... (ma vie sexuelle)* (1996).

9 Except sometimes in Switzerland and Italy, where films are routinely shown with a break in the middle. Intermissions were an established custom in France at the time, but primarily for films longer than two hours, in the large cinemas and the prestige first-run houses. So *2001*'s intermission was culturally overdetermined, as it emphasised the operatic aspect of the film. In recent years, an intermission (lasting a mere two minutes, during which Ligeti's *Atmosphères* was played) was restored for the DVD release from Warner Bros.

10 See my theory of the *acousmêtre* – a character who talks but remains invisible, an acousmatic master and being (this word plays on both the

French *maître* and *être*) – in my book *The Voice in Cinema*, and also later in this book.

11 William Kloman, quoted in Agel, p. 302.

12 In fact, a 'prologue' is actually the moment when one 'speaks before' (the beginning of the action, and addressing the spectator), as in Greek drama or in Shakespeare (for example, *Romeo and Juliet* or *Troilus and Cressida*).

13 In the sense in which 'vertical' is used in western classical music: referring to harmony.

Chapter Four
Style

In the pages that follow, I shall not be considering *2001* as some sort of perfect formal system whose elements – sound, image, directing of actors, sets – complement and fit perfectly with one another. Once again, any 'unitary' conception of *mise en scène* or art is alien to my approach. This section, in a few brushstrokes, will merely attempt to compose a portrait of Kubrick's unique work.

Hero-spectator and Spectator-heroes

2001 is a film whose hero could be the spectator – maybe that is why its characters are so neutral, so we can slide into their skin. They are less *characters* than *tourists*, especially in the second section. The original ads often sounded like pamphlets from a travel agency: 'Imagine you are in *2001* ... your day starts like so.' The film did take on the flavour of a widescreen documentary in the publicity campaigns, and some critics held this against it, but it was part and parcel of the strategy (remember that Kubrick was a reporter for a long time).

We should not forget that the film was shown in many Cinerama theatres, and this giant-image process, formed from three vertical images projected side by side, was associated in the public mind with travel movies and spectacular attractions. The Cinerama spectator was invited to fly over Niagara Falls or the Grand Canyon, or, as with today's techno-spectacles in World's Fairs and certain museums, to experience in his or her seat the sensations of a downhill run on a bobsleigh or a roller-coaster ride.

Both like and very unlike the Cinerama hype, print publicity for *2001* offered viewers not a dangerous adventure with its strong sensations, but a comfortable stay and a pleasant, even hypnotic voyage, and, as icing on the cake, a sort of slow-motion ride on a Ferris wheel.

Kubrick often makes his characters into spectators, even tele-spectators, thereby playing on our fascination for images within images. From the apes gathered around the black slab, to Bowman's eye that seems to paint seas of colour into what it sees, not to mention Poole and Bowman who, while eating, watch their own picture on the screen and listen to their recorded selves on the BBC, characters are often *looking at the same thing we are*.

Characteristically, the only shot in *2001* in line with conventional science-fiction imagery delights in showing us three astronauts in space-suits in the foreground posed against a lunar landscape in the background. But one of them is holding something that looks like a camera, and the touristy aspect of the presence of men on another planet is ironically suggested. It becomes acceptable, and does not seem out of joint with the film – at the same time that it foreshadows the ultimate reduction of Dave to an *eye*. Similarly, a little later, we see the astronauts walking towards the excavated monolith in their spacesuits; they look like a busload of tourists left to their own devices for a few minutes at the pyramids at Giza.

We could also add the flickering video monitors whose palpitations and twinklings undermine the cold calm of Kubrickian imagery that surrounds them. It was a new idea at the time to portray screens within the screen; at least, it was new to use them so systematically. Since then, these sub-screens that Kubrick helped introduce, and which in his films have the peculiarity of often being vertical in format, like portrait paintings, have become baseline props in countless movies.

A Film Laid Bare

In its final form, *2001* approaches what we might dream of as pure cinema. But we have already seen that the director did not get there in a straight line. The process involved adding a lot, and then taking away a lot – without knowing what lay beneath – to attain this bare film.

Anyone who has watched or supervised the editing of a film has felt that at some point, at a stage when the final sound has not yet been laid in and the cuts are rough, the work can attain a sort of mute and mildly hermetic perfection, an irrefutable laconicism, with the obviousness and also the fascinating obscurity of a found object. After that point, whether you are called Kubrick or Joe Smith, what you generally do is go over the work, make things explicit, forge interconnections, extend subtle relations of meaning and rhythm.

Most of Kubrick's films are supported by a voice-over narration, so that where this voice is absent is where 'objectively' it seems the most imposing: in *2001*. Today we find it easy to judge a voice-over as absurd or redundant. But it is hard to know what *A Clockwork Orange*, *Full Metal Jacket* or *Barry Lyndon* would have been without their narrations, which are very explicit or at least which seem so.

Besides, 'narration' has not completely disappeared in *2001*. At times it comes through Richard Strauss's imperious music, like a finger pointing to the determining importance of this moment or that, and narration is manifest, too, in the particular succession of shots.

So it seems that Kubrick had planned at the outset to make this *Space Odyssey* a film of continuities, a film like others whose splices, breaks and matches are covered or absorbed. Ultimately, not only did the director reject Alex North's music, but he put in some of the most dissimilar musical pieces imaginable. In a similar vein, he used the soundtrack to accentuate discontinuities between shots, especially with some moments of absolute, radical silence over shots of humans in space. And finally, he rejected clarifications, so that on the level of articulation as well as story, through juxtaposition of titled sequences, *2001* is one of the barest films in existence – in other words, where the technical principle of fabrication through a collage of moments is accentuated, like exposed wire, like the plumbing and electricity visible in a house whose interior walls have yet to be built.

Settings: a Centripetal and Circular Space

The most remarkable characteristic of the interior sets of *2001* is that, despite the hugeness of the constructions they persuade us to imagine, their perspectives, proportions and lighting immediately give the sense of an enclosed and self-sufficient place. This leads Michel Ciment to observe that the characters 'live ... as if they are holed up in honeycomb cells that do not communicate'.[1] Maybe this helps to explain the heightened sense of drama in certain scenes where one character invades the space of another: for example, when Dave goes to Hal's brain or circuit chamber.

Often in Kubrick, the camera presents interiors – an office, an instrument panel, even sometimes a character – in a way that makes them appear self-contained. The lobby of the Orbiter Hilton, the conference room where Floyd gives his speech, the monolith excavation pit and the Regency bedroom seem offered to our vision once and for all at the instant in which they appear, each like a box of characters. Even the monolith, when the apes first see it, is presented whole, in a setting itself enclosed like a theatre stage. For other directors, such as Hitchcock or Bresson, the image is centrifugal: it constantly points to what it does not contain and what is external to it. The image in Kubrick, in contrast, is very clearly centripetal, attracting attention to what is at its centre.

One factor contributing to this phenomenon is Kubrick's propensity for showing the floors and ceilings of the sets in forced perspective, often employing wide-angle lenses to take in the whole set and surround the characters with it. Kubrick insistently uses long shots that show us the actors from head to foot, a technique used infrequently in sound films.[2]

The director embroiders several variations on this theme. While his curved set for the space station interior is a long 'ribbon' whose extremities we cannot see at any given moment, and scattered with commercial logos and symbols (the Hilton, Howard Johnson phone booths), but including windows on to space, the set of the Clavius conference room is like a hermetically sealed square box, bereft of any signs except the American flag.

The symmetrical conception of certain places reinforces this sense of enclosure. The film's largest set, for example – a combination of models, normal shooting and effects – is the underground airport of the Clavius moon base. Not only do we see it in its entirety all at once (instead of having it revealed to us progressively through editing or camera movement), but also its symmetrical form, filmed from a position emphasising this symmetry, closes it completely in on itself, and with it the vast artificial world it contains.

The circular hallway of the centrifuge where Poole runs like a squirrel in its cage also emphasises the idea of enclosure – contradicting the feeling of euphoric dilation of space produced by the wide-angle lens, which we know makes it look as if a character is going large distances.

Much of the Discovery set is conceived to associate weightlessness and circularity.

Light and Colours: White, Red and Black

As I have said, enclosed spaces in Kubrick give off their own light, enclosing the characters in a sort of aquarium. The toilets and bathrooms in *The Shining*, the bar in *A Clockwork Orange*, Hal's brain, the Hilton hotel and the bedroom and bathroom of *2001* all have walls that appear to radiate light.

White is found almost everywhere in Kubrick's films, and not just in the bathroom settings he is fond of, where important scenes take place in *Dr Strangelove*, *Full Metal Jacket*, *The Shining*. This insistence culminates in *A Clockwork Orange*: the white cats, the white outfits Alex and his companions wear, the enriched milk they drink, the decor of the 'molocho bar', the white phallus-sculpture, and so on. In *2001*, the white sets literally radiate; the audience bathes in light from the screen.

Red is the second important colour. For reasons more symbolic than scientific, *2001* encourages us to see some settings as representing the interior of the human body. This effect is particularly noticeable for the underground area of the moon base, and in the airlock where Dave manages to get back into the Discovery.

Black: in contrast to the many brightly lit images, some shots show the total darkness outside in a terrifying manner. In the scene where Bowman recovers Poole's body, the images and soundtrack bring out the immensity of the void where the action takes place: the pod piloted by Bowman, and the floating spacesuit containing Poole's body, are depicted as tiny dots of matter and light in an ocean of silence and blackness. It is on purpose that the light from the stars in the sky is dull – the symphony of light at the end is then all the more impressive.

Camera Angles: Heroes Turned Upside Down

Low-angle shots are classically used to magnify foreground objects on several occasions in the film, in very specific cases:

- to show the monolith in conjunction with the sun (but in contrast, the first view of the monolith is intentionally 'realistic', and the slightly high angle situates it in a setting clearly indicating its modest proportions);
- when the apeman has worked out how to use the bone and goes about smashing the tapir skeleton; and later, when he triumphantly throws the

bone into the sky. We have a case here of a rather disquieting connotation of the heroic;

- at the beginning of the Discovery episode, when Frank Poole is exercising. This is one of the film's bravura shots; the camera is behind or in front of Poole, and the centrifuge turns around him, situating us in a self-enclosed world where there is no up or down.

  Interestingly, the authors of *Le Foetus astral* note, 'When Dave [an understandable mistake on their part for a movie whose characters are almost interchangeable: it's Frank] shadow-boxes his way around the circular hallway of the Discovery's cabin, and when the camera is travelling ahead of him then follows him, even though he is running, he remains in place: any movement is cancelled out';[3]

- when Dave goes to disconnect Hal: Dave appears at that moment like a sort of menacing giant. But later, inside the brain, he looks more like someone swimming in an aquarium.

Several camera angles in *2001* function to emphasise the fact that we are in outer space. When the stewardess walks on the ceiling (and is thus apparently filmed by a camera riveted to another part of the spaceship), she is shot upside down in the next shot; the camera does a 180-degree rotation to put her 'right' on her feet.

The interior of the Discovery's centrifuge is first presented with the camera on its side, so to speak, on the perpendicular, so that we see Poole jogging horizontally. Another spectacular shot makes Dave, seen vertically, coexist with Poole in bird's-eye view; it shows them in contiguous but different spaces, at a 90-degree angle from one another.

When Poole and Bowman eat side by side, we see them from a high angle, almost upside down.

For all these striking camera positions, *2001* nevertheless adopts a strong horizontality most of the time, including when it shows the silent course of the Discovery, whose elongated shadow, like a snake or a dinosaur skeleton, skims along horizontally, always from left to right, in conformity with the conventional spatial iconography to signify movement towards the future. Similarly, the monolith is to the right when Floyd touches it, and when it appears to Dave Bowman at the end of the film.

Shot Transitions

2001 is a film whose shots are juxtaposed through often stark cuts. Fade-outs followed by fade-ins are rare: the 'Dawn of Man' section has two, there is a rapid one at the end of Floyd's interview with the Russians, and one at the end of the central sequence of the Discovery. But most major transitions are articulated by cuts. The sole dissolve, which we shall discuss later, superimposes Hal's eye over a shot of Dave moving towards the 'brain' to destroy Hal.

The cut has become the principal type of visual transition in film, as is well known. Since the 20s the cinema has normally softened the jarring force of the cut by integrating it into a well-developed continuity system relying on matched movements and sounds, echoes between dialogue and images, and multiple overlappings among the various layers of the film text, so that the potentially brutal rupture ceases to be noticeable. In *2001*, on the contrary, Kubrick strips the cut naked: the cut becomes a device of *commutation*.[4] And his strong contrasts in brightness – from the deep black of the interstellar void to the explosive white of the spaceships – only underscore the rupture of the cut still further.

In addition, we increasingly find as the film proceeds, especially in its most dramatic moment – the duel with the computer – the tendency towards audio cuts synched with video cuts (cut-cut). Although this technique has become quite ordinary by now, Kubrick's film was among the first to popularise it. It occurs in the scenes that cross-cut between the interior of a spaceship and outer space. The cut-cut underscores the rupture between the two spaces and renders it more violently.

Considering the 'brutality' of the cutting in these cases, it is then all the more striking that the only real action sequence in the film, the murder of Poole, uses editing to elide the act itself (the pincers on the pod's mechanical arms cut the cables to his spacesuit). The film conveys the murder via a series of jump-cuts and then a cut to Poole struggling. The action *per se* has been excised, only suggested, by this cut, or rather by the interval signified by the cut. We have no music or any other preparation to warn us: just a sort of commutation with no trace, between the before and the after of a murder, a murder no one in the film will ever explicitly mention.

Poole is literally assassinated by editing. The scissors that connect things (making a bone into a spaceship) are also scissors that kill.[5]

Scene Construction: Face-to-face Confrontations as Impossibility

Kubrick's film employs classical film grammar, but in a very personal and selective way. We can see at the crux of its style a notion of the shot–reverse shot pattern as an impossible face-to-face encounter (except in death), or in any case an encounter approached asymptotically.

To begin with, in the prologue, there are absolutely no shot–reverse shot constructions where we might expect them. We see the head apeman notice the presence of an object, but the next shot, which reveals the monolith, also includes the ape tribe, and is not shot from the angle of his gaze; there is a 90-degree change in camera position. This type of shot transition occurs again at the end, when we see Bowman on his deathbed raising his hand towards something, and then at a 90-degree shift, what he sees, but again he is included in the shot. (It should also be mentioned that the monolith is first seen from the side and then frontally.)

One principle frequently used for dialogue scenes in *2001*, especially in the second half, is the master shot that lays the groundwork for detail shots filmed from the same angle. This creates a general feeling of frontality, even when Kubrick does change camera position. The film uses this construction for all the group scenes: the apes, Floyd and the four Russians in the Hilton bar, Floyd's speech and the group of astronauts in front of the monolith.

The first shot–reverse shot in the film is very symbolic, since it corresponds to a non-encounter: it is when the flight attendant in the Orion returns Floyd's pen which he had let go. Floyd is sleeping and therefore cannot return her look. There are no close-ups in this scene save for the shot of the stewardess's special shoes.

Shot–reverse shots depicting characters in confrontation appear for the first time in the space station, and often they occur between long shots. In *2001, there is not a single shot–reverse shot of two close-ups of human characters*; these are reserved for the confrontations between Hal and Dave.

For example, in the scene with the Russians, the isolated shot of Smyslov pumping Floyd for information does not get the response of a close reverse shot of Floyd answering him, but rather a wide shot with Floyd in the middle of the group that also includes Smyslov. The same thing happens when Michaels asks Floyd a question in the Clavius conference room. Michaels is isolated from the group in a medium shot; a reverse shot then gives Floyd's elusive response. But this so-called reverse shot shows not only Floyd but also his audience, including Michaels from behind. In both these cases, the editing does not 'return the ball', and eludes any crystallisation of either difference of opinion or agreement – these 'reverse shots' give us none of the usual reciprocity between two persons.

Thus the shot–reverse shot pattern is monopolised entirely by the relationship between Hal and human beings.

This system creates absences and tension. Let us consider them more closely.

Hal as panoptic and invisible

Hal can see, and several times we see subjective shots from everywhere through his red eye (circular, distorted images made with a fisheye lens), but he himself is invisible as such. He has 'an eye' or several 'an eye's, and this Cyclopean eye is placeless.[6] The paradox of the numerous subjective shots 'seen' by Hal in this film is first, that they belong to a problematic subjectivity, and second, they can belong to eyes that it is not always possible to locate precisely.

This is all the more evident when at a given moment we literally enter Hal's head (into his circuitry), in order to establish that this centre is empty and that the voice does not come from any precise location, any more than the different isolated eyes are connected to a central overseeing eye. The red eye that fades and goes out when Hal is unplugged is merely one among others. The consciousness is noplace, the source of the voice is noplace, Hal's eye is noplace (since they are everywhere, and since the scene construction and the characters' actions accustom us to this idea without our thinking to wonder about it).

In the scene where Poole and Bowman have broken audio contact with Hal in order to talk privately, Kubrick shows us one of Hal's eyes in the background of the image with the two astronauts in the foreground: the eye is always present. There is no way to visually shut Hal out, and it appears that he can see anything we see.

Certain wide shots of settings, of the centrifuge and the pod storage bay and even one of the instrument panels that contains a Hal eye, are thus capable of being from Hal's perspective too, even if they are not fisheye shots, for Hal's voice reigns over them. *Panoptic* films, whose characters are or believe they are filmed from everywhere, have a tradition in film history. Panoptic films run from Chaplin's *Modern Times* (1936) to *The Truman Show* (Peter Weir, 1998), through *Dossier 51* (Michel Deville, 1978) and *The Osterman Weekend* (Sam Peckinpah, 1983), and *The Thousand Eyes of Dr Mabuse* (Fritz Lang, 1960).[7]

The panopticism is even more striking in the scene of the broadcast from earth to the Discovery, where we see in one image various monitor screens plus the TV show with Martin Amer and, in the middle, an eye of Hal's. These images containing the computer and its interviewer in one shot remind us of Hal's centralising role and of his capacity to 'multitask' or deal with several situations at once. The very first time Hal speaks in the film, that is, when he says 'Good afternoon' during the programme, his eye is present in two forms in the same image: the original, and the filmed image transmitted to a screen.

(By giving Peter Sellers several roles to play in *Dr Strangelove*, and previously a role involving disguises in *Lolita*, Kubrick had already been working with the idea of ubiquity, as he does here with Hal.)

No shot–reverse shot between man in space and those watching him from earth

In the characters' communications with earth, we never see the space voyagers as they are seen from our planet. We do not see Floyd as his daughter sees him, nor do we see Bowman and Poole as seen from earth, except for the TV close-ups that are transmitted to them and that are seen by them.

Poole and Bowman (relatively) interchangeable, since no shot–reverse shot occurs between the two

The apparent interchangeability (despite their physical differences) of the Poole–Bowman pair is partly owing to the fact that we see no shot of Bowman from Poole's point of view, and vice versa. (The only exception occurs in the impersonal form of the spacesuit.) When the 'Jupiter Mission' episode begins, the two crewmates are isolated by both the action and the way the sequence is put together. They are first presented to us separately, each doing his own thing: one is exercising in the centrifuge and the other is simply shown arriving there. Then Dave, having assembled his meal tray, moves to the table next to Frank, but both astronauts watch television side by side like an old married couple who no longer need to talk to each other.

In this scene, each has his own screen to watch, and the editing pointedly isolates the men into separate shots. When they are eventually both in the same shot we see them almost from the back; and the only times they turn towards each other are in the TV programme itself – a programme they watch without registering any reaction to their own image. The next scenes show them separately: when Frank receives the birthday message from his parents, Dave is sleeping; reciprocally, when Dave shows his drawings to Hal, Frank is taking his turn to sleep.

When each in turn exits the spaceship in a pod into the void, with the other keeping track of the operation from within the Discovery, they exchange no radio messages. The two forays into space, treated symmetrically (even if the second ends tragically), occur without speech.

So we have to wait until the business with the AE-35 antenna unit, and the doubts about Hal's functioning, to see the two actually interact. At that point the framing and editing associate them: sometimes we see them together in the frame, sometimes they appear in separate shots but turn their heads toward each other.

Thus subjective shots are the exclusive reserve of Hal, that is, of the hypothetical consciousness of a machine.

In several of his films (see also *A Clockwork Orange*), Kubrick makes both a banal and idiosyncratic use of the subjective shot: at issue is whether there is a gulf or a communication between objective and subjective shots. This is the mystery involving the question of understanding the other. Just as Anthony Burgess tried to enter into the skin of the other (the monster) when he wrote the novel *A Clockwork Orange*, so the character of Hal, through whose eye we see, challenges us to put ourselves in his invisible 'skin'.

In several of Kubrick's films, we are thus placed in the uncomfortable situation of being both invited in and kept out.

For example, the usual agency with which we identify to enter into a story is either a cordial first-person voice-over narrator or a colourful, individualised protagonist. But Kubrick posits his identification-characters as perverted (*Lolita*), monstrous (*A Clockwork Orange*) or mad (*The Shining*), in relation to whom we do not know how to position ourselves. Alternately, he makes the main character dull, opaque and without personality, so that we cannot slip into his skin to partake in the film except for some moments, and we cannot orient ourselves to the story through his reactions (*2001*, *Barry Lyndon* and to a certain extent, the 'ironic' character of Mathew Modine in *Full Metal Jacket*). This does not count those strange third-person narrators who take us by the hand at some points only to leave us in the lurch at others (*The Killing*, and again *Barry Lyndon*).

Shot–reverse shot with Hal and Dave implies a missing element (the face of Hal) and the elimination of one of the two

It is only when the confrontation between Hal and Dave occurs that *2001* becomes a film where two beings face off – but something is still lacking, since there is a face on the one hand, and only a faceless eye on the other.

It should also be noted that this eye of Hal is framed tightly or at greater distance in the *mise en scène* according to the moment, set in a vertical rectangular frame;[8] sometimes we see the instrument panel of which it is part, and the eye is situated in reality. But sometimes we do not see it; then the eye is decontextualised, and Hal's look vanishes into the eye.

Sometimes what it 'sees' is reflected in the eye; in other words, apparently both shot and reverse shot are in the same image. The first time Dave appears in the film, for example, he is a reflection in what we do not yet know is one of Hal's eyes. In a similar vein, a superimposition between Hal and Dave will mark the beginning of the scene in which one of them executes the other, as if they cannot coexist.

In an article published in the magazine *Bref*, I wrote about this moment:

> If you consider only the isolated sequence, you will say that the purpose of this dissolve, in terms of the diegesis, is to signify a simple temporal ellipse (there

has to have been time since Dave's re-entry to the spaceship for him to have put on his space helmet). But keeping the whole film in mind, we remember that there were already other superimpositions of Hal and Dave . . . in which the man is reflected in the eye of the computer/Cyclops, when Dave is conversing with Hal. In these superimpositions it almost seems as if the man's image is being eaten by the machine's ocular globe (the watcher dominating the watched). Coming after several such superimpositions, the evanescent dissolve Kubrick decides to insert at this crucial point, here an effect of narration and not a diegetic effect, also takes on the meaning of a substitution implying the imminent end of Hal. Henceforth the two of them will no longer appear in the same shot, and the man is the one who wins, in an imaginary (specular, in the Lacanian sense) duel. By putting the computer to death, the man takes its place – such that, logically, it is he in turn who in the course of events will become an eye, almost bodyless, swept up into a fantastic voyage.[9]

The reverse shot of Dave, after the death of Hal, is simply himself later in time

Bowman could also reckon, in the Regency bedroom/cage, that he is being watched by people he cannot see (in fact, these people are us), but when he does see someone else, it is himself. The bathroom mirror in the final sequence is the only mirror seen in the film (if you rule out Hal's eye).[10] It also refers back to the monolith, which is reminiscent of a large full-length mirror . . . in which you see nothing.

The only classic shot–reverse shot constructions of the film with actual over-the-shoulder shots along the axis of action occur when Dave, alone in this absurd apartment, seems to see someone, but this someone is himself, either in a mirror or at a later stage of getting old. Until, that is, the cosmic face-off of the final image confronts the Star Child and a faceless planet.

In this final sequence, we are misled by the effects of editing.

At its beginning, a shot of Dave's eye, then his face, is followed by a reverse shot of the room seen from the pod porthole. Then a shot of the eye, and another reverse shot of the room seen from the porthole – but this time it contains an astronaut in a spacesuit. This astronaut is Dave 'later', but he has not been given the time to get out of the pod: it is a mental projection of the image of Dave.[11]

Then this 'other' man in a spacesuit, whom we eventually identify as a prematurely aged and wrinkled Dave, goes towards the bathroom. A subjective shot explores this bathroom. We then see Dave ... but it is his reflection, for the 'original' is partial and out of focus, on the right of the screen. Soon after Dave has seen himself in the mirror, we hear a sound of cutlery on china, indicating the presence of someone else. These sounds, which suggest the solitude of a large dining room in a vast house, act as if to quiet the surrounding reverberant din, but Dave's breathing sounds continue for a little while. Dave turns around slowly. We see successive shots of Dave moving about, and images of the bedroom seen from the bathroom; thus we identify the moving shots as his point of view. The moving camera in this 'subjective' shot, to the accompaniment of Dave's breathing, comes to rest on a character in a robe, seen from the back. In an interminable shot, this character turns around, rises, goes to the bathroom (towards us) as if he too had heard something. It is Dave, still older. This time, the breathing sounds have ceased.

The two Daves turn towards each other, but at different ages and in separate shots.

It is like a father you can never meet again.

There is no 'monolith's point of view'
Finally, the monolith is visible, it can also be touched, but we do not know if it sees – there is no shot 'seen' by it (when a single shot would be enough to subjectivise it).

2001 is therefore predicated on perpetually implicit face-to-face confrontations which are perpetually eluded and deferred. The direct encounter with the extraterrestrial that the film causes us to expect never occurs.

Overexposed Subjectivity
This leads me to re-examine the question of subjectivity and objectivity in Kubrick, as critic Mario Falsetto has done though in different terms.

Let us begin with the fact that the shot–reverse shot figure occupies a central place in film language everywhere in the world, to such an extent that films not employing it are the ones that stand out. For example, there is the magnificent *Sayat Nova* by Sergei Paradjanov, and most of Hans-Jürgen Syberberg's works. However, of course, their conscious omission of it is yet another form of using it as a point of reference.

In *Sayat Nova*, characters are filmed looking directly at the camera, as if for individual and group portraits. This 'camera look' nevertheless constantly implies a reverse shot, that of our 'screen look', so to speak, so strong is the model that makes each film image a potentially subjective image, that is to say, susceptible to retroactively being transformed by the following image into 'an image seen by X'.

The cinema is unique as an art that can subjectivise the objective; it has the ability to give to an object that is shown, whatever it may be, the status of something 'seen by . . .'. Likewise, cinema can objectivise the subjective, that is, it can take a perception that is given as subjective, and render it a framed object, situated in space and in time.[12]

Kubrick is *not* one of those directors, which include Paradjanov, Syberberg and Manoel de Oliveira, who tend to refuse this perpetual beat back-and-forth of the shot–reverse shot pendulum. He maintains this structure as central, but in a highly personal way that disturbs its functioning. Instead of conserving its usual ambiguity, its intentionally insidious quality, he overplays or overexposes it. He does this by fabricating images we might call *overobjective* – endowing them with a precision that exceeds the needs of editing and narration – and images that are *oversubjective* – marked strongly as being 'seen by', either by the way they are edited in (Dave's eye, the things he sees), or by the exaggerated foregrounding of usual signs of subjectivity: wide-angle distortion (like the images seen through the judas holes in a door), the hand-held camera, a first-person voice-over, and so on. Kubrick sticks to 'classical' film language, but he casts it in a stark light, and thereby makes it problematical.[13] Kubrick's films question before they affirm or negate, because they strip the cinema bare in its workings.

This sense of bare exposure applies to all the cinema's elements: overplaying or underplaying by actors (two sides of the same coin), baring of the scenario's form and its articulations, overexposure of music as an appropriated text.

From One Strauss to the Other: the Music Cues

Because of the shock produced upon *2001*'s release by the choice of the 'Blue Danube' Waltz to accompany the first two outer-space sequences – a shock that was felt as pleasant and also curiously intoxicating – *2001* is a film that is mentioned frequently in discussions of film music. In fact, in my book *La Musique au cinéma*, I devote several pages to this one film alone.[14]

In one sense, *2001* behaves like a silent film in the way it appropriates and adapts pre-existing musical pieces. On this level it succeeds to a degree that Kubrick would never again attain: magic formulas are rarely a sure thing (I consider *The Shining*'s music a disappointment).

But with *2001*, his seventh feature film – only after he had ordered a score composed, and later abandoned, did Kubrick find his chosen way of using music. It consisted in placing the music 'outside', in other words, not mixing it closely in with the dialogue and sound effects, but using it in broad, autonomous swaths, often borrowed from pre-existing works, songs or classical pieces. The film's numerous *silent* scenes also give Kubrick's vision the same opacity, the same obtuse and enigmatic presence, infinitely open to interpretation, as a musical theme.

Accounts of the genesis of the film confirm that in the initial plan, numerous dramatic sequences, including the murder of the three hibernating astronauts, were supposed to have music, whether borrowed or original pieces. These are precisely the scenes that have no music in the finished film. Little by little, Kubrick refined an approach that reverses the usual formula: most of the action passages such as space walks and murders go without; the music seems to be reserved for contemplative sequences.

Let us also note that when *2001* came out, only a tiny minority of filmgoers knew the music of the contemporary composer György Ligeti. You could find his name by attentively watching the closing credits, but most of the audience would get up and leave the cinema, as they still do today. It was possible to believe, then, that they were witnessing a work or rather a sound-effects composition that was created expressly for the film, especially since at certain points the director actually mixed sound effects with the Ligeti music.

The same is true for the Richard Strauss excerpt, which most filmgoers discovered thanks to the movie, and for the little-known Khachaturian interlude. Thus it is only with the 'Blue Danube' that Kubrick produced culture shock – even while denying it, as he claimed that the young audience would bring to this waltz no historical association whatsoever.

Cultural connotations provoked by music can vary enormously according to the era, the country, the film audience. Today the problem is the reverse: it has become difficult for many people, myself included, to hear the 'Blue Danube' Waltz without thinking of spaceships.

With his symphonic poem *Also sprach Zarathustra* (*Thus Spake Zarathustra*, composed in 1896), Richard Strauss tried to translate into music some of the themes expressed in Nietzsche's text, and the score's opening two minutes that Kubrick used (out of a total length of about thirty-five minutes) is called 'Sunrise'. However, the triumphant effect of this music *in the film* seems to me no more tied to Strauss's title and the content of Nietzsche's work than the title of the 'Blue Danube' is tied to the idea of a central-European river and the colour blue. A musical piece that is 'borrowed' and integrated into a film is not some sort of enigma whose key can be found once you identify its title, its composer or any programmatic associations it carries. If Kubrick had chosen a different part of the same symphonic poem by Strauss, which is a collection of very diverse musical moods in terms of style and tempo, it seems obvious that the meaning of the sequence would radically change.

The opening musical phrase of the piece acts almost like a jingle, irresistibly reminiscent of the musical fanfares of the big movie studio logos. It memorably begins with a long, low, 'primitive' sound, and then turns into an ascending theme of extreme simplicity (doh-so-doh), the most basic intervals in music: perfect fifth, perfect fourth, octave. The vertical and triumphant quality of this theme immediately strikes the listener, and its effect seems to be universal in doing so.[15]

Then comes the play of meanings that is normally created by the restatement of a theme through different scenes, meanings that accumulate and form a discourse. In *2001*, we hear the same fragment of music in relation to different kinds of images: of grandeur (stars and planets in orbital conjunction, the triumphant apeman in low-angle shot, the Star Child as big as a planet), but also of aggressivity and destruction (the ape's jubilation in smashing the skeleton). The music thus wordlessly narrates all the ambivalence Kubrick wished to convey; for him, in this tableau of evolution, the exaltation of life and joy of destruction are inextricably linked.

His next film, *A Clockwork Orange* was even more explicit in this regard. It showed how Beethoven's Ninth Symphony, a message of peace and cosmic exaltation (even if we ignore the lines of Schiller in the sung text), can be associated with the most shocking scenes – rape, wars of conquest, suicide – and that this works just as well.

We might say that the musical form of the fanfare, as both a glorious and tragic announcement (or both at once) runs through much of Kubrick's cinema. For example, a synthesizer is used in many a passage in *A Clockwork Orange* and *The Shining* for fanfares; and of course, fanfares play a major role in Alex North's score for the biblical epic *Spartacus*. In a sense, the fanfare reminds us that all Kubrick has done is make movies about war and hunting (in different forms), certainly films that always have predators and prey.[16]

The *Requiem* for choirs, soloists and orchestra by the Hungarian-born Austrian composer György Ligeti (born 1923), which is heard with each of the first three appearances of the monolith, and which on the third occasion segues into an orchestra piece also by Ligeti, *Atmosphères*, was composed between 1963 and 1965. Again, it is not the title of the piece that counts here, or the sung text – *Kyrie eleison*, 'Lord, have mercy' – which is not intelligible in any event. What we do remember from it is the feeling of its vast, continuous choral crescendo in rising and falling undulations. It can be heard either as a collective lament, owing to the continuous sliding by half-tones of the interweaving melodic parts, or as an attack or threat, because of the sense of a crowd or mass, or even as an eschatological anticipation (in other words, waiting for a sacred event), culminating in high chords. It would be a betrayal of the effect of this piece to try to close off its resonant chains of signification by trying to assign a more precise meaning to it.

Listening to this part of the *Requiem*, it is impossible to decide if this is a human sound or not, instrumental or not: an ambivalence entirely fitting for the ambiguity Kubrick sought.

The recording style popular in the 60s for contemporary music consisted of diluting the sound in heavy reverb, either during the recording itself or added in the mixing via an echo chamber. Such is also the case for this version of Ligeti's *Requiem*, in the spirit of a period that loved all-enveloping, floating and diluted forms, and against the grain of what would be 80s tastes. Kubrick would not have achieved the same effect with a more recent, more analytical recording style, with the dry acoustics that allow better discernment of the instrumental and vocal parts.

Regarding his much-discussed choice of the 'Blue Danube' for the space sequence (some people told him this waltz would create parasitic associations with orchestras in grand hotels and Viennese operettas), Kubrick declared, 'Most people under 35 can think of it in an objective way, as a beautiful composition. ... It's hard to find anything much better than "The Blue Danube" for depicting grace and beauty in turning. It also gets about as far away as you can get from the cliché of space music.'[17] It is surprising to think that the music he originally tried out for this passage, and almost adopted, was the Scherzo from A *Midsummer Night's Dream*. Although this piece is also very rhythmical, it goes at a more rapid tempo and its sonorities are much freer, lighter, like gossamer. This case illustrates yet again how many possible solutions might exist in scoring the film.

According to Andrew Birkin, the Strauss waltz came as a gift from the gods. 'In fact, this choice came about completely by chance. The projectionist had fallen asleep and had let the film run while his radio was on ... Stanley really showed his open-mindedness and was able to seize the opportunities that presented themselves to him.'[18]

But in fact – and here we must add a clarification that will always come up in speaking of film music – Kubrick did not use the 'Blue Danube' Waltz *per se* as much as a specific recording of it by the Berlin Philharmonic, a recording characterised by the sumptuous, capacious, mellow and homogeneous sonority obtained by Herbert von Karajan. The piece comes in only twice during the story, during Floyd's two space flights; but we remember it better than the other music because it is associated with the first images of the future that the film gives us. Aided by the waltz, the film treats the space flights as sequences in a silent film, since there is nothing else on the soundtrack. Characters move and even talk (in the second flight between the space station and the moon), but in silence.

At the same time, this silent image creates a certain discomfort, a sense of emptiness and luxurious coldness, characteristic of Kubrick and appropriate to the mystery he weaves. Something is missing in all this dancing plenitude. I cite Kubrick's use of the 'Blue Danube' as an example of what I call *anempathetic music* – music whose ostensible indifference to the situation on screen, implacably continuing no matter what, creates an expressive contrast. We can also see a suggestion of eroticism in it, thinking of the penetration of the spatial wheel by the Orion rocket. In the world of *2001*, as at the beginning of *Dr Strangelove*, only machines make love.

Several of the silent shots we see with the music of Johann Strauss are taken from scenes that originally were to have dialogue. In the screenplay, the captain of the Aries did not just join up with Floyd but spoke with him; similarly the stewardess, the captain and the co-pilot originally exchanged some lines.

The total absence of sound apart from the waltz also gives to the round ship Aries an insidiously menacing quality, in the way it sends out its pseudopods like claws and 'looks' through the two eyes of its portholes. This subtly animal quality, like a stalking feline, is very important in the film. The forms of the film's space machines and vehicles may be dictated by technological and practical imperatives, but at the same time they have pincers and jaws to catch things, eyes that survey and mouths that can crush.

Kubrick also insisted on dialling up the 'Blue Danube' a third time in the closing credits, like a parade, though he reserved the Ligeti *Atmosphères* for orchestra for the intermission.

The 'Blue Danube' for orchestra is not just a theme and a waltz rhythm; it is also a story. In the version of the 'Blue Danube' that was chosen, what is important for the startling audiovisual match that jumps across four million years is the string tremolo that starts this cue, and which resounds like a First Noise. In this Karajan recording, Johann Strauss's music itself tells the story of a double genesis: a melody from the simplest notes of the scale, and a rhythm from a tremolo. The three central pieces used in *2001* – the dawn of *Zarathustra* and its Arpeggio, the opening of the 'Blue

Danube' on the perfect major chord and the 'Kyrie' from the *Requiem* – have ascending motion in common, in their melodic development and in their dynamic crescendi. This contributes powerfully to giving the film its optimistic character.

After *2001*, Kubrick would go for funeral marches instead, in *A Clockwork Orange* as well as in *Barry Lyndon*, while *The Shining* begins with an arrangement of the 'Dies Irae' by way of Berlioz and Wendy Carlos. Or, as we have seen, he does a parodic and/or ironic number on luminous and joyful music in *A Clockwork Orange*. From this perspective, *2001* would be his last positive film before *Eyes Wide Shut*.

The short excerpt from Ligeti's *Lux aeterna* for a capella women's choir magically plays over the shots of the moon bus going towards the Tycho crater and the monolith therein. If it bears a precise relationship to the 'Kyrie', whose restatement it precedes, this is not necessarily because it was also composed by Ligeti, but mainly because it too is based on an unintelligible singing voice, and on a sort of shimmering of high notes on the edge of formlessness. But here, the female voices are in the high register and they are heard reverberating as in a church, transcendent. The *Lux aeterna* is the closest thing to religious music heard in the film, reminding us perhaps of the messianic emphasis of some science fiction.

The Adagio from *Gayaneh*, which marks the opening of the central episode on the Discovery, consists of slow, dreamlike song, played almost exclusively in the strings, with some notes from the harp. *Gayaneh* is a folkloric ballet in four acts, composed in 1942 and reworked in 1952 by the Soviet composer Aram Khachaturian (1904–78), its 'plot' combining amorous rivalry and political struggle among the Kolkhozians. The work was long unknown – except for the ultra-famous sabre dance of the fourth act (a classic of circus and music-hall) – until Kubrick took its beautiful Adagio which is inspired by popular Armenian music.

This melancholic interlude illustrates how contingent film music really is, since it does not allow us to forget, as we hear it over the images of the Discovery, that all sorts of other pieces of music would have been possible. And this is what Kubrick wished. This piece helps to give the scenes a discreetly poignant sense of solitude, but it still does not become one with the images. It remains apart, alongside, creating an atmosphere all by itself. Its meaning does not stick, does not completely impress itself on the image.

So we have here two very distinct cases. Richard Strauss and Ligeti become indissociable from the scenes in which they participate; they seem to impregnate the situation and in turn be impregnated by it. Conversely, Johann Strauss and Khachaturian tend to slide or refuse to stick to the image – and our emotional response depends on the slightness, even the fragility of the audiovisual association, whether happy or melancholy. Meaning does not completely 'take', which is why there results a heart-rending feeling of contingency and evanescence.

What is certain is that, in the choice of this excerpt from *Gayaneh*, Kubrick sought a strong contrast with the preceding sequences of inter-planetary travel. From the whole symphony orchestra we move to strings only, from major to minor key, and from a dancing totality to a forlorn song. By gradual degrees, the film has drifted to great distance and solitude, preparing for our passage to other worlds.

The uses of the 'Blue Danube', the *Lux aeterna* and *Gayaneh* have some points in common: all three are associated with specific travel sequences, and all obey the same structure, as each cue is divided into two parts to frame a dialogue scene. The 'Blue Danube' Waltz accompanies the word-less sequence of Floyd's voyage, *Lux aeterna* the flight of the moon bus towards the monolith and *Gayaneh* the exposition portion of the Discov-ery mission. The fact that none of these music cues recurs elsewhere (except for the 'Blue Danube' in the end credits) reinforces the role of each as a marker of a sequence and of a particular atmosphere.

On the other hand, *Zarathustra* and the 'Kyrie' of the *Requiem* run through the entire extent of the film and unite the outlying sections, the first being associated with the idea of conjunction of heavenly bodies and of triumph, the second with the presence of the monolith.

Intervening on two occasions, in the intermission (when a screening has one) and then in the 'cosmic trip' sequence, Ligeti's *Atmosphères*, com-posed in 1961, is an astonishing orchestral piece on the threshold of formlessness, close to what could be imagined as the sound of matter in continual transformation. It is like one single sound that slowly evolves; sometimes individualised sounds emerge from it, and even clear sustained notes of trumpets; at a certain point this sound reaches its height in strident flute sounds, before plunging again. Certain sonorities that resemble electro-acoustic music are created on a piano by two players who directly manipulate the strings with such materials as brushes, brooms and cloth. In choosing this music, Kubrick may have been attracted by the notion that the listener has a hard time telling what s/he is hearing (classical instruments? synthetic sounds?). At the same time we cannot assign any precise representational meaning to these sounds that would render them 'sound effects' in association with the images, which could help give the image too precise a meaning.

In a good many other films made before or since, synthetic sounds have become as irremediably dated as the electronic instruments used in the 50s for films like Hitchcock's *Spellbound*. Kubrick thus made a truly inspired decision.[19]

Aside from that, what do all these pieces of music have in common? The commonality is precisely that they are completely unaware of one another, as much through their stylistic differences as their historical eras, their instrumental colour, their sound – in other words, in all respects. Where Alex North's score, through its symphonic unity, would have tied together the different parts of *2001* (which would have yielded a completely different work), the samples of borrowed music both tear the film apart, isolating its different parts from one another, and create its unity through their very incommensurability.

A Drama of Sounds and Voices: Towards Silence

Sonically speaking, *2001* is a stripped-down film, despite the stereophonic sound that is used to greatest advantage for the choral and symphonic musical excerpts.

The way the film deals with voices – and remember that dialogue occupies a mere 42 minutes of 160 – is very subtle and resides in small differences of tone, resonance, accent. No one raises his voice, let alone shouts; the slightest stumble, the least note of exasperation in a line thus becomes very noticeable. We find this, for example, when Poole allows himself to become impatient with Hal, who has been reiterating his accomplishments ('Of course I know all the achievements of the 9000 series'); or when Hal repeats himself ('Just a moment, just a moment'), he who normally speaks without redundancy and in fluid and detailed phrases. The three accents heard in the film are Russian, American (the Americans and Hal) and English (the BBC anchor and interviewer); in general, Kubrick has avoided full-bodied and richly timbred voices. This strategy lies at the other end of the spectrum from *Dr Strangelove*, which has some enormous voices (George C. Scott) and some strong accents (Peter Sellers). The prevailing idea here is ordinariness, naturalness and professional efficiency. This is life from day to day, and just because the characters live in 2001 (a mythical and distant date in 1968), they are not going to take on a solemn, sententious tone.

However, slight differences contribute to animating the film and creating a fabric of sounds and voices.

Anyone who has 'audio-viewed' *2001* remembers the absolute silence in the shots of movement through outer space. It is important to note that this silence exists only for certain very specific shots (no more than two or three minutes in 160), and that Kubrick renders it unforgettable by leading up to it gradually.[20]

First, for the effects and ambient sound heard inside the spaceships, *2001* uses quite a modest vocabulary. Taking a cue from the famous *Forbidden Planet* (which had the audacity to eschew instrumental music, and whose 'stellar' ambience was created by a mix of electronic sounds created by Louis and Bebe Barron), *2001* avoids avalanches of blips and beeps, and its ambient sound is simple, consisting of insect noises in the prehistoric section and varying degrees of air hiss and engine rumble in the spacecraft. Each setting has its own sound or has none at all, like the Clavius conference room which is totally silent.

The equally restrained use of beeps and alarms for dramatic purposes is confined to two scenes, both without dialogue: when Hal murders the three hibernating men, and when Dave re-enters the Discovery through the emergency door.

For the sequences of space travel, when the camera is filming from without like an eye floating in the void, Kubrick appears to apply a simple principle faithful to physical reality: since there is no sound in a vacuum, there will not be the slightest sound linked to operations or movements of machines.

So what is heard over these many shots 'taken from' outer space, shots in
which the camera shows a space flight or an astronaut working in the void?
Kubrick develops a pattern that progresses through the film as follows:

1. To begin with, we hear *orchestral music* (Strauss, Khachaturian) to solve
   the problem: this music bathes the whole of the sequence, interior and
   exterior shots alike, without any other sound of speech or noise in the
   exterior shots.
2. Then, after Dave Bowman's sortie and for all the scenes in space attire,
   we hear the *breathing* of a cosmonaut in his helmet; Frank's death is thus
   dramatised when we no longer hear it. Over the breathing is superimposed a constant high hiss. This can represent the cosmonaut's oxygen
   flow – but can also suggest, when Dave (in his spacesuit inside the Discovery) disconnects Hal, something that is being implacably drained of
   its air.

   The first time we hear these human breathing sounds, which exem-
   plify what I call objective-internal sound, is in the shot before the initial
   foray into space and where Dave, having put on his spacesuit, walks into
   an airlock.

   Note that the hiss that continues over the entire scene in outer space
   does not get interrupted when we cut to Frank inside the Discovery. So
   we are not sure whether Dave is being heard by Frank by radio or if
   there is a slippage or mismatching between the point of hearing (in
   Dave's helmet) and of the point of view (in the Discovery). This
   example indicates the complexity of questions of *listening* (the audio
   equivalent of spectatorship) in film.

   The breathing sound is both reassuring and disturbing, as if our head
   were in the maw of a lion. We can discern slight changes (for example,
   when Dave opens the panel containing the antenna unit), but never any
   pronounced or noticeably identifiable variations that might emphasise
   one audio moment more than another, or a particular physical effort or
   gesture.
3. The arrival of *absolute silence* in the film corresponds to Frank's demise.
   (Until this point, as I have said, shots from the 'point of view' of the
   void were accompanied by music, or by objective-internal sound.)

Frank's death is subtly anticipated in the soundtrack by a slight inten-
sification of the air hiss over the series of jump-cuts showing the pod
approaching.

So Frank dies, and all shots from then on which show the pod and
Discovery from outer space, after eighty minutes of preparation, are
seen in absolute silence. *Except for one moment*: a strong dramatic
licence is taken briefly when we hear Dave's 'on-the-air' voice calling
Hal from his pod, trying to get a response: 'Do you read me, Hal? Hal,
do you read me?'[21] These words and the beginning of Hal's answer that
follows are the sole words heard in space during the entire film. After
this, the dialogue continues over the images of the two adversaries,
never overlapping: the eye of Hal in the Discovery, close-ups of Dave's
face inside the pod.

A very common audio convention today, when the script has an
exchange of messages over the airwaves, calls for human chatter in the
midst of static and radio noise while we see exterior shots of planets or
spaceships. We hear this in *Alien* and many other films, but actual news
footage has also trained us to expect this. None of this occurs here.
Besides, in *2001*, when one astronaut goes out into space and the other
remains in the spacecraft, with his spacesuit partly on and in visual contact with him (a situation that occurs twice), they do not deem it
necessary to say a single word. Just as on the visual track the
shot–reverse shot figure is used only for Dave–Hal dialogue, the
exchange of dialogue in space is also reserved exclusively for this pair.

4. Finally, for the last section, when Dave's pod is taken in charge by an
   invisible force and the 'cosmic trip' begins, the dense and diffuse music
   of Ligeti's *Requiem* returns. This is mixed in with rumblings that could
   well be a motor – thus a sound in the void. But of course, all notions of
   realism or unrealism become irrelevant. After all, we have already
   accepted that a static camera is stationed in space, and is 'watching' the
   Discovery go by like an eighteen-wheel truck on the highway.

Nevertheless, Kubrick's example became a point of reference; it seems
to have created an immutable rule for sci-fi soundtracks. So when Ben
Burtt's team of sound designers set out to invent sound effects for *Star
Wars*, they were at a loss when faced with this taboo that decreed no sound

in space. Until, that is, Lucas officially gave them permission to break it: let us treat space as if it were air, he told them. And that is why spaceships began to rumble again like tanks or roar like racecars (since another Lucas innovation consisted in showing spaceships move around five times faster than anyone had done before).

To sum up the audio scenario of *2001*, the second and third sections gradually bring on more noises and gradually take out music.

For the two sequences of the Orion and Aries (going toward the moon), the only thing heard is the symphonic version of the Strauss waltz; we are in a technological universe that is unnaturally silent. The two parallel scenes of Floyd's discussion with Smyslov and Floyd's speech to the scientists on the moon allow us to hear only either extremely subtle ambient sound or none at all.

The first time we hear sounds associated with movement in space occurs inside the moon bus. In that scene muffled sounds can be heard, with the rhythm of a sort of secondary pulse like a pump, on top of the music of the *Lux aeterna*, which is gradually decreasing in volume. Later, at the beginning of the Discovery section, the Khachaturian music mixes in much more with speech and noises in the ship, with the footsteps and panting of Poole as he exercises, and even with the warm chorus of Poole's parents as they sing 'Happy Birthday' – without truly fusing with them, however, since the Khachaturian retains its own rhythm and space.

After that, music disappears from the soundtrack for a long time (aside from the short BBC music logo), not to return until the spectacular cue of the third reprise of the Ligeti *Requiem* in the following section, 'Jupiter and Beyond the Infinite'.

It is in the section richest in action that the 'orchestra pit music' (or non-diegetic music) stops, once it has led us into the year 2001.

Hal and the Humans: Voices and 'I-voices'
The voice of Hal would be justified in receiving a whole chapter of its own. I have written about it in my book *The Voice in Cinema* as an example of both an *'acousmêtre'* (a character who exists as an acousmatic or invisible voice, with no place and supposedly able to see all, know all and do all), and an 'I-voice'. I call the 'I-voice' (so named because it resonates in us as if it were

our own) a voice outside a film's spatial reality, with no acoustical indices of distance or direction that might situate it in an identifiable space. The I-voice, in order not to be contained, is itself a container and insinuator.

Hal's voice possesses all these properties, and Kubrick takes care to have Hal's voice closely miked, with no spatial indices or reverb, while the voices of other characters are often heard as if at a distance, or reflected off walls inside the ship. The reverb on Bowman's voice, for one, varies in different spots of the Discovery centrifuge, and thus the voice gives credibility to this set as a real space.

In the confrontation between Hal on the Discovery and Dave in the pod, Dave's voice, even when we are in his pod, is distant and weakened, to underscore his position as David against Goliath. Hal's voice, on the other hand, is 'spaceless', with the same soothing and ubiquitous presence no matter where it is.

When Dave, back in his spacesuit and helmet, disconnects Hal, and when he speaks briefly to tell Hal to sing, the man's voice sounds lightly filtered, suggesting transmission through some technical means, in contrast to his breathing, which remains close and present.[22]

Returning to the scene of Poole and the recorded birthday message, we should note that three levels of voice meet. The parents' voices seem distanced and diminished by the transmission; they are heard with no reverb. The voice of Hal, when he adds his 'happy birthday' to Poole, is warm and close (this is the first time we hear Hal 'live' rather than in the TV programme). And the voice of Frank, who is the only character present in flesh and blood, is slightly reverberant as if in a catacomb, suggesting the funereal atmosphere of this necropolis flying through space that is the Discovery. Hal and the human characters, then, belong to strikingly different sonic spaces.

From one end of the film to the other, we do not hear in Hal's voice a single physical indicator of breathing, swallowing, throat-clearing or anything else that I call *materialising sound indices* – and this helps make it disembodied (the opposite of the harsh, grating voice of Alpha 60 in Godard's *Alphaville*). Incidentally, it is impossible not to admire the quality of Douglas Rain's diction: he maintains a remarkable balance between smoothness and pedanticism, firmness (even authority) and seductiveness, gentility and aloofness. In the brilliant scene of the computer's death, this voice has an unforgettably dreamlike quality and seems mentally to take leave of itself (the way Rain repeats the name 'Dave ...'), and its phrasing is impressive, for example when it says, 'My mind ... [silence] . . . is going.'

No one forgets the little song the computer sings as it is dying. The idea came from Arthur C. Clarke, who had heard a computer sing it in the 60s, using one of the very first synthesized voices. 'A Bicycle Built for Two' was written in 1892 by Harry Dacre, one century before the birth of Hal:

Daisy, Daisy
Give me your answer, do
I'm half crazy
All for the love of you ...

In this tender and naïve song, the suitor dreams of riding a tandem with his beloved Daisy. As Hal sings it in the film, it slides inexorably downwards to indicate the death, or loss of consciousness, of the computer.

The technical device used (and fairly well adapted in the French dub, I might add, where the voice was made to sing 'Au clair de la lune') did not consist in simply slowing down the recording of Douglas Rain's voice; this would have slowed down the tempo as well. Only the pitch and the timbre change, while the rhythm remains constant.[23] To obtain this effect in 1968, before the effects made possible by computers, Douglas Rain sang several versions of the song at faster and faster speeds, after which, in the editing stage, the rerecording was done at slower and slower speeds. Thus his voice always remains at the initial tempo, but plummets lower and lower and gives the effect of a record playing at ever slower speed. At that time not so long ago, when the compact disc did not exist (and would not enter the market until the early 80s), it was a familiar experience, and even an amusing pastime, to put a 45-rpm record on at 33 or vice versa, and to play with record speeds – impossible today with commercial digital players. We must add that a 'digital' slowdown that can be created with computers today would not have yielded as good a result, because the electronic texture of such digital manipulations would be too obvious.

Acting and Mood: Solemnity and Spontaneity

2001 is a film that reputedly was acted in an intentionally neutral and cold manner throughout. I would simply like to suggest here that the story is rather more complicated and, in the restrained palette the director chose, the smallest nuances count.

The acting is certainly restrained but it is not insipid. The complexity of our response results from the subtle relationship between framing and action, between camera style and performance.

A scene such as Floyd's speech, if watched in isolation, is little but Kubrick ironically observing a social ritual (pleasantries, scattered applause), shot by a static camera. However, if we compare it with the scene that follows – the men's conversation in the moon bus – we see that it constitutes a stage in a gradual progression.

The later scene, where Floyd, Michaels and Halvorsen look at photos of the monolith over coffee and sandwiches, seems merely to extend the preceding one by supplying new plot information. However, there is a subtle and simple variation of style and atmosphere. First, when the scene opens on the bus interior, the camera moves, which it has not done for a long while, in a slightly unstable dolly-out (almost as if hand-held) from the cockpit back through the cabin. The actors, headed by William Sylvester as Floyd, set a different tone from that of the preceding scene: here they are more like cowboys in a Western chatting around a campfire. They have lost the formal stiffness they had in their business suits. Now in their spacesuits (without helmets), they look like robust, direct, pragmatic Americans.

The whole scene is arranged so that its momentous revelations (this object is not from the moon; it seems to be an expression of a non-human will) are made in the most quotidian tone, in an atmosphere both cordial and reserved. The dialogue packages these astonishing revelations in simple, familiar formulations: the unearthed object is called 'the damn thing'. When Floyd/Sylvester smiles at the idea of a monolith 'deliberately buried', he does so like a scientist intrigued by a new problem, relishing the work ahead. These men we see are research specialists who are travelling on the moon. They are not going to move around with dramatic pomposity in a solar system they have learned to approach as a field of study and a series of scientific challenges. Kubrick's choices here are guided by his concern for truthfulness; the film aims to show how we might approach the problem if we were in their situation.

As for the scene of the discovery of the monolith – the first scene filmed – it is simply admirable for the manner in which it was conceived as well as the manner in which it was executed. For this first contact shown between human beings and a mystery from outer space, the director strikingly combines solemnity with spontaneity. The solemnity is conveyed through the processional character of the cosmonauts' descent into the monolith excavation pit, to the sound of the deeply moving music of Ligeti which in this context could almost represent a multitude joining the men and pressing against the wall of the object (which is shown from above, as in the beginning of the film, and not like a sacred monument shot up against the sky). The spontaneity is obtained by the (apparent) use of the hand-held camera, which does us the favour of bringing us into the group by adopting the point of view of one of the astronauts, letting us see over his shoulder as the men walk towards the monolith. There is spontaneity also in the group's loose meandering towards the slab; they move in relative disorder, and the gesture of one man inviting his compatriots to pose for a picture feels completely spontaneous. Likewise, Floyd touches the surface of the monolith with his hand, in a shot that is both extraordinary and without stiffness. It shows the story's central mystery, but not imperiously. Such a treatment heightens rather than diminishes the scene's grandeur.

In other cases, the natural discretion of the scenes reinforces how simply moving they are. I am thinking of the programmes and messages recorded or relayed from earth, all of which have elements of spontaneity. Floyd's little girl squirms and fidgets and scratches her back; Dave and Frank before the BBC cameras begin with a bit of hesitation and a little laugh (Kubrick may well have decided to use an out-take); and Poole's parents whisper to each other in the middle of their weekly message that they know is being recorded. This spontaneity, boxed up and framed like a portrait, like a snapshot that reduces a life to the dimensions of a portable photograph, moves us and speaks to us as only truth can do.

The Movie's Concept: Careening away from Earth
The paradoxical notion of making a film about 2001 where 2001 would be

a year like any other seems to have haunted Kubrick and inspired his desire
to mix seamlessly the everyday with the futuristic.

For example, the concept of the entire second section, which introduces
us into the future (the flight on the Orion, the arrival at the wheel-shaped
space station), is to show the extraordinary as ordinary. We are going to the
moon, but it is a routine flight and no one is surprised to see a ballpoint
pen floating in zero gravity. The pen is just the futuristic equivalent of an
object that, when dropped, you return to its owner. To accentuate the
banality of the future, an announcement about a sweater left by a lady in
the Orbiter Hilton restaurant is heard twice in the space station ('A
woman's cashmere sweater has been found').

When Floyd arrives at the station, the first sentence heard in the film
establishes normality: a hostess says, 'Here you are, sir.' Floyd's first gesture
is to close the zipper of his small portfolio (in Tarkovsky's *Solaris*, the corresponding scene is more burlesque: the astronaut who arrives in the space
station trips on his own shoelaces and falls on his face). Then, various 'Good
mornings' assure us that in space, people go by the same clocks as on earth,
as well as its formulas of politeness: 'Did you have a pleasant flight?'

The set for the station includes vast picture windows through which the
rotating earth can be seen, but no one looks at the show, let alone comments on it in amazement.

The little girl Floyd talks to from his 'picturephone' booth – Kubrick's
own daughter Vivian, who later would make a documentary about the filming of *The Shining* – seems posed in place like a doll; you would think she
had always been there before the conversation ever began.

During his phone call, Floyd raises his voice, as the first telephone users
did, and the little girl's voice is filtered. We hear no bleeps or futuristic
sound effects accompanying the actions of dialling a number, making the
connection or hanging up.

During the conversation the girl, wearing a pretty princess dress, fidgets
and is only barely able to sit still. It is amusing to note the many lateral or
vertical reframings to keep her centred in the frame (a vertical frame, the
format of an identity photo), which would lead one to suppose that in the
world of the film there are robot cameras that can follow people who are
on the videophone.

The conversation between Floyd and his daughter has no delays between questions and responses. This is the first stage in a series of communications that will underscore the progressive movement away from earth. Later, in the recorded programme Bowman and Poole watch while dining from their trays, spectators are told that there was a delay of seven minutes between the interviewer's questions and the answers, and that this delay has been edited out. Thus the spectator is made more aware of the recomposed, artificial character of the interview, all the greater because the invisible Hal is participating and can rival the interviewer with diplomatic and stereotyped formulas. But communication is still bilateral at this point.

Later still, Poole receives the recorded message from his parents, which seems all the more pathetic and touching in that visually it only occupies a very small subsection of the screen (except for one brief insert shot). The soundtrack contrasts its demonstrative warmth with the oceanic serenity of the Khachaturian music. Here, communication is no longer reciprocal. The parents send the message as an audiovisual letter to someone whose reaction they will not see. The distance the camera obliges us to take from the scene (a distance also created for the sound of human voices which gets lost in space) and the presence of the Khachaturian music that over-arches this sequence are the two elements that 'refrigerate' this affective warmth.

As for the content of the birthday message, it reminds us of the everyday, earthly aspect of Poole's life: he has bills to pay, he is an astronaut at such-and-such a level. But all this is presented in such a dry, impersonal mode that we do not remember any of the information we are exposed to – there is nothing in it to want to hang on to. Additionally, the fact of the birthday underscores that we are in a world where counting time in hours, days, months, years is nothing more than a convention, maintaining earthly rhythms in a universe that does not recognise them.

Each time, the size of the subscreen showing the character 'in communication' gets smaller with respect to the size of the screen itself. Little Vivian is shown closer up than the BBC interviewer, and in turn the latter is shown closer – except for a brief shot – than Poole's parents.

Floyd's video briefing, also unilateral and prerecorded, seen just after Dave murders Hal, has no close-ups. Floyd is but a small dot in the vast movie screen, and the video image flickers so much that we no longer even know who we see in the image; it is hard to be sure it is Floyd.

These final communications with earth are messages from people who no longer 'see' the characters. The very last one is even set off automatically, without taking any account of the tragic reality of the survivor who receives it.

But these people all speak without grand words and in the same cordial and professional manner. Everyday reality recedes farther and farther, but with no drama or emphasis. Very gradually, the film leaves behind the shores of the ordinary.

Rhythm: from Slowness to Rupture

By comparison with the roaring speedboats that modern sci-fi films frequently are these days, *2001* is a slow-paced film, moving along like a grand ocean liner of yesteryear. But this tempo is necessary to change our perception, to adapt it to a new space. *2001* is a film that accustoms us to outer space, and is accordingly very gradual in its rhythm.

Other films, beautiful though they may be, often take us on our visits to the galaxies like hurried tourists. We hardly have time to see the landscape and to feel what the billions of miles mean. Who other than Kubrick has tried to make us feel what it is like to live in a world where there is no up or down? *2001* gives us time to shed our usual spatial and temporal orientations; to go round with the characters, not just watch them go round as gawkers at a country fair.

Of course, this slowness in *2001*, particularly noticeable in the second section (the voyage to the space station and the arrival on the moon), can be maddening for those who do not easily settle into the film. The same goes for the static quality of the more sterile scenes (Floyd's conversation with the Russians and especially his speech on Clavius),[24] scenes whose expository character Kubrick accentuated rather than disguised.

Similarly, it is without the slightest haste that Dave disconnects Hal and we see his memory circuits leave their housing. And the sound of Dave's breathing, hardly accelerated at all at this tension-fraught juncture, contributes to regulating our own rhythm as spectators.

The slow pacing also has to do with the image format. *2001* is conceived for Cinerama cinemas, where the size of the screen is itself a sensory event. Stereo sound, in the magnetic sound version, is also an experience in itself which allows for a slower rhythm (as Tati for his part attempted to do in *Playtime*).

The time of the projection is thus transformed into a ritual.

Entire sections of *2001* are devoted – uselessly in terms of suspense or the progression of the plot – to the act of moving from point A to point B, as part of a mission. In much the same way, *Dr Strangelove* is constructed from the alternation between interior scenes (where for varying reasons characters are isolated and shut away) and scenes of a mission, such as that of the bomber. And the shots of Halloran in *The Shining* going to the Overlook Hotel, alternating with the scenes inside the hotel, are full of pathos, particularly when you consider that he is going to be killed instantly.

Kubrick strongly emphasises the dead time sometimes involved in going from one place to another. He often refrains from adorning it with any action whatsoever. It thus becomes a sort of ritual in itself, a long preparation for a moment of breaking or rupture. This break occupies only an extremely brief moment – more than brief, a non-moment, a *commutation*.

Notes
1   Michel Ciment, *Kubrick*, p. 107.
2   But which is found in numerous films of the 50s and 60s made for giant screens, such as Todd-AO and Cinerama spectacles.
3   Dumont and Monod, *Le Foetus astral*, p. 149.
4   [By this term, which Chion has adapted from the French word for an electric switch, *commutateur*, he means an abrupt, instantaneous switch. – Translator.]
5   An ambivalence that I have already found in David Lynch who, like Kubrick, is obsessed by the question of immortality. See my book, *David Lynch* (London: BFI, 1995, trans. Robert Julian). The cinema is the art of ambivalence *par excellence*.
6   Just as towards the end of the film we see Dave's eye in extreme close-up during his 'cosmic trip'. Being limited to one eye (like Hal before him), he loses the psychological connotation of the 'look'. Later, on the other hand, in the scene of the Regency bedroom, Kubrick shows Dave

from head to foot and returns his body and his look, thereby strongly soliciting our identification with the character – but all the better to trap us. There is apparently someone else Dave hears and sees, but this someone else turns out to be himself at a later age, and we are thrown back out, obliged again to interpret rather than identify with him.

7   [The panoptic text has perhaps reached its millennial apogee in TV reality shows such as *Survivor* and *Big Brother*. – Translator.]

8   The vertical frame for the eye echoes the shape of the monolith.

9   *Bref*, no. 42, Autumn 1999.

10 Dumont and Monod emphasise the sequence in the Discovery where Poole and Bowman watch themselves on television: 'this show is the only "mirror" into which the men ever look during their trip toward Jupiter' (p. 87). But do Poole and Bowman see themselves in Hal's eye?

11 I am suggesting that the astronaut we see could at this moment be Dave-seeing-himself-in-advance-where-he-is-not-yet, in a mental representation of his future.

12 Considered this way, sound plays an ambiguous role, for it is much more difficult to situate a sound as being subjective rather than objective, or inversely. We never know if a character hears what we hear, and if we hear what he hears.

13 Journalistic rhetoric, unfortunately too often used in scholarly research, which talks in this case of 'subversion', 'corruption', and so on, seems to me to be the least intelligent way to understand this process and ignore the dialectic that subtends it (and whose supposedly 'subverted' system comes out necessarily reinforced).

14 Michel Chion, *La Musique au cinéma* (Paris: Fayard, 1995), pp. 345–52.

15 Its 'primitivist' quality is equally due to the unsubtle sounds of the timpani. The gesture of the apeman beating with the bone, which we see during one of the cues containing this musical piece, suggests the gesture of a percussionist – which Kubrick had once been.

16 In this connection, one of the other temp tracks used by Kubrick during the editing of *2001* was, characteristically, Mahler's Third Symphony. This piece has numerous fanfares, but also a chorus and a *lied* for soprano and orchestra on a text of Nietzsche's *Zarathustra*.

17 Agel, p. 88.

18 *Studio* (Paris), no. 144, April 1999, pp. 118–19.

19 *Musique concrète*, of which I am a practitioner, is difficult to use in film, contrary to common belief. The sounds it brings into play have a marked tendency to take on too realistic a signification. It would be rather like using the contents of a Pollock painting or a Brancusi sculpture as parts of a movie set.

20 As I shall show in the paragraphs that follow, first there is the full audio spectacle of the symphony orchestra, then a more rarefied musical sound (*Gayaneh*'s strings), then a single, simple sound (breathing) and finally, silence.

21 My term 'on-the-air' describes sounds present in a scene that are supposedly transmitted electronically (by radio, TV, and so on) that are consequently not subject to 'natural' laws of sound propagation.

22 This is a contrast and a contradiction: we hear the spoken voice of Dave 'from outside', his internal breathing 'from inside'.

23 I thank my American students at the Paris Critical Studies Centre for this observation.

24 Each time I see the film, this scene is hard to sit through, but the function of its tedium is clear in the context of the whole film. Any 'livelier' treatment would throw out of balance everything that follows.

Chapter Five
Towards the Absolute Film

Commutation

Let us revisit the first two appearances of the monolith. The final images of these two scenes, with the sound that accompanies them (in 'The Dawn of Man', a high chord of the Ligeti music, and in the scene on the moon, a very high strident tone), show us the object from a low angle, so that it cuts into the sky; both scenes end abruptly, even brutally, with simultaneous cuts on image and music. The monolith thus becomes associated with the idea of interruption, of immediate obliteration – of *commutation*.[1]

Commutation essentially means that where there was nothing, suddenly there is something, but this something can itself disappear in an instant. This has been the case for a century with lighting by electric bulbs, unlike the lights that came before – candles, oil or gas.

It is a similar story for sound. With the tube amplifier, the sound gradually increased in intensity; with transistor amps beginning in the 50s, sound comes instantaneously, so that when you turn on the dial or press the button, you get music at once.

The ever-increasing speed of modern computers is having the effect of making us insatiable, accustoming us to demand things *right now*. But for more than a century there has existed an art founded on instant commutation, and Kubrick in *2001* is exploiting it as such. This art is the cinema.

Film editing can be seen not only as a way of constructing or stitching together, but also as a series of commutations that make a visual state disappear instantaneously (and also an audio state, as soon as that became possible with the invention of optical sound) to replace it with another that means the complete erasure of the first.

In Kubrick's hands, editing characteristically gives us the feeling that there is no build-up of the information supplied in the shots, no memory of each shot in the one that comes after. In many ways, *2001* is a film about amnesia, or something resembling it, which is quite ironic for a speculative sci-fi film set in the future (and therefore implicitly commenting on 'the past'/our present). The various episodes can appear amnesic with respect to one another and the only way they hook into one another is by visual or auditory 'rhymes', which we have to locate on our own, perhaps even fabricate.

For example, among humans there is no anamnesis of the humanoid apes who were their ancestors. The human of the year 2000 is shown, *like* an ape, living in families and in groups, sleeping, having children, eating and defecating – in other words, in his pure and simple functioning as a living species, with no reference to culture.

Similarly, though curiously for a movie that has this title, the fact of going into the third millennium and thus of taking part in a collective symbolic history hardly seems to preoccupy the characters. This is especially true of the two Discovery astronauts: constantly occupied with immediate tasks, in fact occupied with maintaining their minds (the 'nice renderings' of Dave's drawing, Poole's chess game) or their physical bodies (Frank Poole's jogging and his tanning session) in good working order, the two men live in a sort of continual present or in any case a short-term one, never raising the issue of where they have come from or where they are going. Only Hal mentions – and in such abstract terms! – a 'mission' to carry out, but finally he himself dies, regressing and activating the memory of his very first vocal message ('Good afternoon, gentlemen') – so we would seem to have an anamnesis, which literally means loss of forgetting – but in fact, since he forgets what made him Hal, this is literally a memory that is emptying itself, and does so without trace.

A strange and unique masterpiece, this film: it proposes to be a perpetual here and now, and a purge of memory – leaving room for the future – even as its action spreads out over millions of years and millions of millions of miles in space.

So it is up to us to construct this memory, to fill in these holes, to make a work out of this void and to place an inscription, if we wish, on the nameless stone slab.

The 'Before' and 'After' of a Wordless Non-event
Aboard the Discovery, Hal the computer questions Dave about his confi-

dence in their enigmatic mission. Dave neutrally replies that everything is
fine; then he asks Hal: 'You're working up your crew psychology report?'
Hal answers in the affirmative and excuses himself. Then, after a repetition coloured with haste and a slight quaver (he who usually speaks
unhesitatingly), the computer announces (falsely, as we shall find out later)
that a crucial antenna part is about to stop working. Something has come
undone in Hal, a threshold has been crossed, with no audio or visual sign
to mark it. It happened in a period of silence, without memory. There is a
'before' of the moment of Hal's slipping, and an 'after'. What happened
to the moment itself?

The playing of chess accustoms us to dissociate the mental strategising
from the physical move itself. The first, the mental work, is invisible and
is normally represented in comics by wheels or gears turning inside the
player's head. The act is symbolically irremediable and on the visual level
negligible, a mere detail, which consists in playing one move among others
contemplated. In chess, you have made ten moves in your head before
choosing the move you do make, and there is a sort of gulf between the
important stuff that happens – the invisible, unsituable and traceless
moment of the choice – and the symbolically significant and irrevocable
gesture that is the actual move. For this move has been mentally played
ten times before being 'realised'; its realisation encounters no resistance in
reality. In fact, you can play chess just announcing the moves verbally, as
Poole does in the film, since it comes down to the same thing.

It seems to me that Kubrick's shots are shaped by the idea of an invisible mental process that leaves no traces, which is actualised by jumps in
successive edits. And, just as the chess move that is played cancels and
rejects the other possible choices, the edit chooses one solution and anni-
hilates the others.

In chess the move itself is both an act and a non-act, in the sense that
the time you spend doing it is not what counts. All it does is symbolise a
mental decision. But the decision is impossible to situate by going back in
time, as you notice if you try to pinpoint it. What happens is the creation
of a before and an after, with 'holes', interruptions, that could contain the
moment of the decision or a gap – impossible to pin down.

Later, in the Discovery, the murder of the three hibernating cosmonauts (who did not have the time to become characters for us, and the filmgoer cannot remember their names, even as they are written on their coffins, so briefly did they appear) takes place as a series of beeps and light patterns – the graphs of physical and brain activity gradually flatlining – but in any case, it takes place as a succession of shots marking the before and after of an event with no words.

The sequence is treated symmetrically: a shot of the eye of Hal, several shots of the coffins, then the succession of video messages and physical graphs, then other shots of the coffins, *ever motionless*, then a shot of the eye of Hal as at the beginning.

The two shots of the eye that frame the scene are static and identical – the eye before and the eye after are the same. And Kubrick has intentionally not shown the slowed breathing of the frozen bodies; their life is shown only by the abstract means of biological indices. Death is inflicted like an act outside time. Nothing has changed.

Here, it is we who again must create the cause–effect relations between the eye of Hal and the flashing messages, and project meaning on to these images and their progression. For this reason I do not follow Dumont and Monod when they write that Hal's 'inert eye' 'watches' the hibernating men 'before provoking [alarm signal] their transformation into cadavers'.[2] For 'watches' is already a logical interpretation. Strictly speaking, we do not know if he is watching. We see it, that is all.

The fact that later neither Dave nor Hal utter a word about Frank and the three other victims contributes to the sequence's mystery. The murder is shown indirectly, but is never corroborated by words, and this transforms our relationship to it.

Of course, the message 'Life functions terminated' says what it means, but one observes that already on its terms it is an understatement. And what is shown here is entirely metaphorical. We never see the dead body as such, nor shall we see the remains of the astronauts.

Or later, once the song of the dying Hal has definitively, grotesquely plummeted in pitch, Kubrick leaves no time to allow our emotions to kick in. As insensitively as a TV channel that cuts off the end credits of a movie – or, if it lets them roll, leaves not a second of blackness or silence – Kubrick immediately rolls Floyd's prerecorded video briefing, as if nothing were amiss. Floyd's message was produced eighteen months beforehand, with the understanding that it would not be unveiled until the end of the mission. Since the message itself is unaware of the drama that has occurred, it makes Floyd look like an amnesiac from the past where he addresses Bowman.

Then begins, without the slightest reflection or recapitulation, the trip episode of 'Jupiter and Beyond the Infinite'. The death of Hal has thus also been a commutation, a death with no trace, no body, no eulogy or requiem, purely an effect of editing: the images and sounds that follow do not bother to think about what they are covering or erasing and over what they are written.

Here the movie screen shows itself for what it is: a surface on which none of what lives and pulsates upon it becomes imprinted.

In this sense, the monolith is a participant. It is at once a screen and the opposite of a screen, since its black surface only absorbs, and sends nothing out.

Is there not some connection here with the 'indifferent universe' that Kubrick says is more terrifying than anything else, and which leads us, in order to make it all hold together and make sense, to project ourselves, our emotions, our will to live?

On the other hand, the brutal commutation seems to meet up with what would seem to be its absolute opposite – the long, continuous tracking shots, the very slow progressions (quite possibly the reason the director chose the Ligeti music characterised by gradual metamorphoses, with no rhythmic or melodic centre). It could be thought that these commutations (visual, auditory and psychological) simply work to bring out the long sections in which a phenomenon appears or disappears through a stretched-out gradation rather than all of a sudden: the spaceships' arrival at the space station, the gradual death of Hal, the psychedelic sequence at the end. But the opposite way of looking at this is equally important: the more progressive the gradation, and the more continuity masks any cuts and gaps, the more dramatically a subsequent rupture is highlighted as the product of an enigmatic edit (for example, the enigma of the time between the shots of younger and older Daves in the bedroom scene). The transition from one shot to the next in cases such as this produces an effect of arbitrariness, it appears as a mysterious choice, not clearly justified. This is the very effect of the signifier, because the signifier, defined as arbitrary by Saussure, is here a series of cuts, ruptures, uncrossable barriers.

Discontinuity and commutation refer back to what is for humans the sharpest experience of discreteness: that which institutes the acquisition of language, which – obviously in accordance with its reconstruction *a posteriori* – cuts for ever into the vocal and auditory continuum of the baby's existence. Language is what separates phonemes from sound, but does not manage to rid the sound from the envelope of 'non-pertinent' sound characteristics as from the shell of a chrysalis, and which will always tag along with it as superfluous sound.[3] The shots of *2001* are edited together like the elements of a language or an alphabet, their articulations visible. The film comes across like a text reduced to its hieroglyphic materiality.

And it is in the edit of all edits, that which unites the 'Dawn of Man' passage with the discovery of the future, that this effect is felt the most strongly.

The Edit: Where There Was … Now There Is … Or There No Longer Is

Justly famous, the transition between the bone in the heavens and the heavens of the future takes one's breath away by its simplicity, its grandeur and the overwhelming power of what it signifies. If cinema is an art of the spatiotemporal ellipse, here is one fine example.

Where there was (a horse-drawn omnibus), now there is (a hearse): the legend goes that because he stopped his camera for a few moments, creating this substitution, Georges Méliès discovered special effects. Several of the most striking effects in *2001* are based on the same idea, achieved by simple editing. In the place where there was a bone (that is, in the same place *on the screen*), there is a space shuttle or satellite; later, where there was old and dying Dave Bowman (in the bed), now a foetus is shining forth.

And where there was nothing, now you have – or now you don't – a monolith. (The monolith is identified with the edit itself, with the invocatory power that makes it appear and disappear.)[4]

A snip of the scissors, a splice, and you have crossed over four million years. The object triumphantly thrown upwards by the apeman, who has just discovered the weapon and the tool, is commuted, through a single edit, into an interplanetary vehicle; and from the dawn of humanity we topple over into the space age. In terms of sound, too, everything leads to this single transition, possibly the most famous one in the history of film, certainly one of the most sublime. On the slow-motion image of the bone turning over in the sky, the ape-king's triumphant cry fades down in an airy wind, and once the nocturnal 'future' image of the spaceship travelling through space comes to replace instantaneously the earthly, diurnal, palaeontological one, what do we hear? The film does not just crudely strike up the symphonic 'Blue Danube' Waltz theme, but to begin, there is just the thin tremolo of string instruments, on the threshold of the audible, to introduce the waltz – something like a birth.

However, even if it occurs gently, a commutation has indeed taken place and something important has no less fallen through the trapdoor of the ellipse: all the life on earth in between. Not a single image of the planet inhabited by human beings in 2000, before they took off into space, can be seen in the whole film. The various messages (both live and recorded) received by the humans in space reveal nothing of terrestrial life.[5] Once these messages have been sent from earth, they seem to leave no trace on those who have watched them; no one we see comments on them, let alone expresses any feeling of nostalgia for the life they apparently represent.

The moment of the shot transition itself puts two flying objects in relation with each other. But the movement it conveys began further back and continues on beyond. What we have is a symmetrical trajectory of three objects: a bone is thrown into space by the ape who had held it, it starts to fall; the rocket-object that replaces it on the screen does not fall down, it is a spaceship and it stays up by itself in the air. Finally, we see a pen – same oblong and phallic shape – that floats inside the spaceship, and is returned to its sleeping owner by the stewardess. To the erect and propulsive arm of 'Moonwatcher' answers the floating arm of Floyd who is sleeping like a baby, and in his unconsciousness has let go of his fountain pen. You can see what interpretations could be made of this sequence (of the type: progress softens men), if we were to insist on that kind of reading.

Another aspect of the sequence that deserves mention is the rack-focus

that shows the pen floating against an unfocused background; a refocus-
ing then seems to react to the stewardess entering the cabin, and
immediately shows her in sharp focus. This is the only shot in *2001* to use
a rack-focus, which acts like a direct sexual allusion (the camera appear-
ing to be connected to the woman), in a work from which sexuality is
otherwise evacuated.[6]

The floating pen is also an immediate illustration of the world of zero
gravity. Finally, it is an image of *infinite regression*, it is like a tiny spacecraft
that floats inside a spacecraft which itself floats in the solar system . . .

The shot transition has thus led from an object that falls to an object
that does not fall: it is the triumph of Icarus. The victory over gravity, shown
in this way, produces the giddiness that characterises the experience of the
little human who stands for the first time and walks.

Gravity, left behind subsequently in the two interplanetary episodes,
returns at the end of the film. Although the film did not follow through on
the bone thrown upwards by the apeman to the end of its fall, the glass
that Dave knocks over in the room where he ages falls to the floor and
breaks. A trajectory is thus completed, and the magical edit has not con-
jured away the cycle of decline.

However, because of the edit, for a while a part of what was cast upwards
did not come down. The ellipse created by the edit is not just that of millions of years of evolution, but also that of the very small event of the
bone's inevitable fall to earth: it eternalises, beyond man, a triumph.

The Said and the Shown
Images and Captions in Kubrick

In Vincent LoBrutto's biography of Kubrick, we read that one day in July
1946, during his career as a photojournalist for *Look* magazine, young Stanley saw three of his black-and-white pictures in print, at the end of a humour
article. This photographic minisequence depicted the confrontation
between a chimpanzee and human visitors in a zoo. The first photo showed
the ape alone, and the other two showed what the animal was presumably
seeing: humans behind the bars of his cage. This makes you think of *2001*,
where some invisible barrier seems for ever to separate the watcher from
the watched. Who knows, could the black monolith be a bar in a fence?

LoBrutto adds that the meaning of the first of the three photos (the picture of the ape) was channelled or justified by a caption imposed by the *Look* editor: 'a female monkey looks at men'.

There was a time in magazine pictures when the caption functioned as a link between the particular character of what is shown and the general character of some meaning being imposed. The caption also functioned to 'dignify' the photographed image, while obliging the image to take on (or pretend to take on) a certain imposed meaning (here, the indecipherable look of the animal, and the idea of a reflection on the distinction between man and animal, the power that man arrogates to himself to put creatures in cages, and so on). In a word, the caption made the image 'think', just as man projects his thoughts and feelings on animals.

Today, too, magazine photos are never printed without a supporting text to 'introduce' them. The difference now is that many more journalistic photos are supposedly snapshots of an event, the trace of an emotion, rather than the emblem of a situation-type or a moral. Besides, we find inside the magazine pages of today a proliferation of all manner of headings, intertitles, scraps of sentences taken from the text and placed in larger type as epigraphs; and all this obscures the basic role that was once held by the caption. The text itself is manipulated, laid out, framed, mounted, considered as an object to zoom in on (the use of larger type in a modern page layout is no longer the equivalent of a strong statement, a headline being shouted, but a swelling of words), it becomes almost an image among other images. For these and other reasons, the function of the caption has become diluted in the overall page make-up. The dialogue between the written and the seen is less 'out in the open', more tortuous, more difficult to locate.

Kubrick produced many photos in the 40s that, unlike today's pictures that are so quickly gobbled up, were meant to represent something more general than the moment they were shot. He would photograph a monkey, and the magazine made a picture of the simian condition out of it. It was no longer Kubrick's photo that people would see, but rather what the picture was deployed to 'illustrate'.

In the history of western painting up to recent times, the title or its idea has often pre-existed the painting whose subject it treats. The artist then can decentre the subject if he wants in the midst of a vast landscape or a single architectural space (as in the flagellation of Christ as depicted by Piero della Francesca). Inspired from the painting title, the photo caption, on the other hand, has long claimed to give *after the fact* a general, exemplary, even edifying or symbolic connotation to fragments of life, a connotation that often had nothing to do with it, stealing their own particular meaning and import.

It seems to me that Kubrick's long professional experience of the paradoxical situation whereby the thing that sold and promoted his pictures, what framed and authorised them – that is, the caption – was at the same time the thing that corrupted and limited their meaning, gave him a particular sensitivity to the arbitrariness of this forced meaning by words. He no doubt felt the power and the trickery, and at the same time the fascination, of the mismatch between an image and a title. Even as a title claims to 'bring out' something in the image, it does not open up the image and does not remove its share of opaqueness.

When Kubrick became a film-maker, he seems to have adopted a certain way of using text, whether text to be heard (voice-overs) or to be read (intertitles and subtitles): as if he were sometimes imposing photo captions. Even certain selections of theme music (whose most famous example is the *Zarathustra* excerpt in *2001*) retain this sense of exteriority; they are shown as showing, rather than fusing with what they encaption.[7]

For this it is necessary for what is shown – especially visually shown – to give off a sort of aura, a capacity to imprint itself on the eye; it has to be non-recuperable by the spoken word. Kubrick's perfectionism involves the magnificent and moving quest – most often crowned with success – for images with strong presence, rendering them (at least in part) irreducible to verbal and narrative exploitation and interpretation.

Let us examine examples from two other Kubrick films, *Barry Lyndon* and *The Shining*.

Functions of the Intertitle and Voice-over in *Barry Lyndon* and *The Shining*

Barry Lyndon is also a film based less on the *contradiction* between image and text than on a certain *parallelism* with no hope of a meeting between the said and the shown.

In the image, Barry Lyndon is a specific being, opaque and hardly loquacious, whose singular fate is retraced by the film, while a narrative voice and title cards in silent-film style try to make this fate illustrate a general lesson. Image and text never truly come together. On the one hand this is because of several contradictions demonstrated by Philippe Pilard in his excellent book on the film,[8] but on the other because they belong to different levels and the image was conceived, in my opinion, to close in on itself. By this I mean that Kubrick's image has the capacity to be a place of mystery, not necessarily trying to 'communicate' with other images that precede or follow.

Towards the beginning of the film, Redmond Barry is playing cards with his cousin Nora, and the slightly sententious voice-over narrator comments: 'First love!' then holds forth on love among the young. Listen carefully to this 'First love', and watch the smooth face of Ryan O'Neal;[9] see if this statement works on the image in a Kuleshov effect. I am really not sure. I cannot say yes, but neither can I say that the Kuleshov effect is inoperative. Just as the specific ape became the whole species in the context created in *2001*, here the specific character – as trapped from the outset as the zoo animal photographed by Kubrick – if he serves the narrator to 'illustrate' the emotions of youth, remains as impossible to see into as an animal. But nothing more. For Kubrick the image 'lends itself' to commentary; it does not refuse, but it does not give itself over either. The image is the place of a singularly passive resistance. And do not think that the image's power of passive resistance is easy to obtain.

The 'cage' for Redmond Barry here is just as much the image as the bosom of his cousin Nora whose décolletage she invites him to explore in order to find the ribbon she hid there. We have already seen in *A Clockwork Orange* this image of a man paralysed before a female body that towers above him, when Alex has undergone the brainwashing of the Ludovico treatment, and when he is exhibited to the public as powerless and sexually impotent.

Through its generalising about youthful love, the third-person masculine voice of *Barry Lyndon* hence 'captions' the image in a way that is neither entirely provable nor irrefutable. Let us remember that the novel by Thackeray is told in the first person; this is underscored ironically in the English title *Memoirs of Barry Lyndon*, 'by himself'. Remember also that the mem-

oirs are presented as both collected and annotated by a certain Fitzboo-
dle, who at times gives his own opinions. The very chapter titles curiously
alternate between first person ('I Pay Court to My Lady Lyndon') and third
person ('Barry Leads a Garrison Life'). Thus the novel plays a complex
game on several levels, even if this embedding of narrative levels is less
prominent than in many other eighteenth- and nineteenth-century novels.
It seems that Kubrick, using very simple and unostentatious means, re-creates this ambiguity. But doing so entailed a bitter struggle with cinema and
with the overly easy and obedient image, to become a way of illustrating a
pre-established verbal meaning.

We should note that Thackeray was also an illustrator, who illustrated
his own *Vanity Fair*. I do not know if the role of illustrations in literature
of preceding centuries has been studied as much as it deserves, but it seems
to me that this is a highly important subject: the dialogue between image
and text dates from much further back than the cinema.

The intertitles at the beginning of *The Shining* also have an ambiguous
function. The first title, 'The Interview', just after the credits, seems like
the name for a painting, and in fact it introduces the meeting between
Jack Torrance and the manager of the hotel, played by Barry Nelson. But
in fact this scene is cut up, haunted, by a parallel scene that acts almost
like radio interference, a scene at Torrance's house between his wife and
his son.

The next title, soon after the first one, reads 'Closing Day'. This one is
also presented on a title card, not superimposed on a shot as in *2001*. The
sequence that follows begins with Torrance's car driving his family to the
hotel they will look after for the winter. In comparison with the first, this
title hovers ambiguously between functions of temporal indication and
'genre painting'. The third title, 'A Month Later' (before the famous scene
of Danny driving his little car through the hotel corridor), definitively tips
over into temporal designation. This is like *2001*, whose intertitle 'Jupiter
Mission: 18 Months Later' oscillates between the idea of a painting title
and the function of identifying the temporal setting.

None of this is irrelevant, not even the presence or absence of an article.
'The Interview', like the film's title, has the definite article; 'Closing Day'
has none; and 'A Month Later' uses the indefinite article. Between *the* and

a lie differences that count. In the Kubrick filmography it is amusing to
note two films with *the* – *The Killing*, *The Shining* – and two titles with *a* –
A Space Odyssey and *A Clockwork Orange*, often not translated literally into
foreign languages for distribution abroad. In general, the indefinite article
respects the specific character of the image, while the definite article gen-
eralises it.

The Title and the Film

The resonance of a film's title is not usually a crucial issue. Why does it
become so with a very few directors, such as Fellini and Kubrick? Fellini
justifiably made a fuss because an unfortunate French subtitling job
allowed a clapper-boy to say the title *Intervista* at the end of the film where
the director had intended us to hear something arcane and incomprehensible. For Fellini the title is a magical invocation, a cryptogram, a sacred
name, like the phrase 'Asa nisi masa' in *8½*. With Kubrick, on the other
hand, the title is like a caption for a painting: it brings out the lustre of the
image, beats the drum for it. We sometimes read in his titles words that
could apply to images: shining, full, wide, space, whereas *A Clockwork
Orange*, even though taken from the Burgess novel, is really a painting title,
for a film in which the paintings of Christiane Kubrick play a considerable
role.

   In Kubrick the shock comes from the particular way the image solicits
or asks for a caption, to accept the tribute of a caption, but then to decline
it. I have insisted on the care Kubrick brought to his camerawork, and
would like to insist again on this obvious point. For Kubrick the primacy
of the visual is never to be taken for granted as a 'given' by the very definition of this art. You have to defend the image, each time anew, you have
to magnify it, place it at the centre, make it shine. The symmetrical fram-
ings dear to the director (especially in *A Clockwork Orange*) and which he
emphasises through *mise en scène* as well as through the wide-angle lens
that accentuates the receding perspective lines, do not merely frame the
image in a closed composition, they centre us on to the image. And they
become the centre of the filmic totality, they invite the film's other elements
to gather around the image, but not to enter.

   In Kubrick, the image, well aware that it could get swallowed up by a predetermined meaning, seeks on the contrary to swallow our attention, like the open vagina of the erotic sculptures in the bar in *A Clockwork Orange*. Those provocative sculptures of nude women with thighs spread, leaning on arms and legs, or offering their nipples which gush forth enriched milk, bring out the devouring symmetry of the female body. This seems to me a very apt metaphor of Kubrick's imagery: from the Overlook Hotel to the corridors of the Discovery and the trenches of *Paths of Glory*, and of course to the space of the psychedelic trip of *2001* that splendidly 'offers itself' to us, these are all just containers that devour or spit out characters.

In Kubrick the image is also a feminine phallic body, an armoured nudity. Armed also with its scintillating nudity, it cannot allow itself to be manipulated so easily by sound.[10]

Let us now see how this play of the said and the shown works in *2001*.

A Story without Words?

The prologue of *2001* (as Kubrick completed it, having abandoned the idea of a voice-over) makes a show of telling a story 'without words'. In the guise of a succession of tableaux, not unlike giant dioramas from a wax museum, 'The Dawn of Man' meticulously lays out its concise history of evolution. The image of ape skeletons abandoned on the ground 'tells' us that this species did not yet practise burial (burial would suggest that we are already in the era of human culture). The presence of tapirs peacefully coexisting with the apemen foraging for food places the two species on the same side of evolution for a while, and 'tells' us that the apes are herbivores. The tiger that attacks an ape tells us that this species has a predator, forcing them to live in fear with the imperative to protect themselves. Note the magnificent shot of the tiger standing near a zebra carcass and watching them: its luminous eyes foreshadow the twin lights of space vehicles watching in the interstellar night.

The scene of the horde tells us how important it was to congregate around a watering hole, and suggests an embryonic stage of social organisation. The little pond is also the focus of a territorial rivalry between clans (our first fights are with our brothers, suggests Kubrick), which announces the centrality of war in future human history.

The group at night, listening in the darkness to the noises and growls of beasts, tells us about a universe of fear. A mother and her offspring tell us of the embryonic family; a crescent moon evokes outer space to which later the descendants of these 'animals' will catapult themselves.

And so it goes. Apart from the fact that it is a title (that is to say, words), 'The Dawn of Man', like that of a painting, invites us to see in this sequence a history and not the repetition of a series of specific moments. For there is only history in the dimension of the symbolic, thus of language.

The Mental Image

2001 also poses the question of the mental image expressed without words; the only shots in the film that we can attribute to the *thoughts* of a character are from the perspective of an ape.[11] Dumont and Monod identify two shots, close together: the one of the monolith inserted between two images of the ape considering – or rather momentarily *stopping from considering* – the tapir bones, and the shot of a live tapir falling down.

Significantly, it is when the animal is no longer specifically looking at anything that we take it to be 'thinking'. But to 'see someone thinking' is a phrase that underscores a paradox of cinema.[12]

Film can move right up to a face or head, but cannot go inside. It seems as close to subjectivity as could be, but it can only present subjectivity through objective means. It retains an unavoidable opaqueness, and heightens the impenetrability of what it claims to reveal. Film mimics interiority, and denounces it as a deception at the same time.

In this very example, what presents thought as visual (and why not?) is not the conscious representation of the ape character, but its unconscious. It is not the monolith, but an image of the monolith seen from a certain point placing it on the axis of the sun – and even more than the image of the monolith it is the *shot* of the image of the monolith, with its particular framing. Kubrick is taking on the impossible task of bringing to life Eisenstein's dream of conveying abstract thought on the screen through purely visual means.[13]

In the same scene we also see, twice, a deliberately stylised slow-motion shot of a tapir collapsing. The shots act as both a memory and a flash-forward; they are both a mental image, conventionally attributed to a character's perspective, and objective reality, showing what happened (the monolith now gone) and what is going to happen (the live tapir that is going to be killed). Third, the shots indicate the ambiguous intent of the film, which deliberately neglects to clarify their narrative status. Is it the narrator speaking (to tell us, 'this ape has seen the monolith and will kill tapirs'), or the character thinking in images?

Out of these first ambiguous mental images is born abstract thinking, and subsequently the power to send objects into space.

The tool is a mental projection. Similarly, the spaceship, the future and the sky also appear to be mental projections, both possible and realised.

These mental shots become relayed still further into the future by 'virtual' images, graphic productions based on antennas and radar, seen on control monitors when a spaceship approaches its destination, and is preparing to land or take off.

To translate the role of the monolith into visual imagery, Kubrick initially planned to superimpose on to an image of this object some hypnotically suggestive shots showing carnivorous apemen instructing the apes. Deciding against the use of superimpositions – which were common in the silent cinema – as well as verbal explanation via a voice-over commentary, gives still more importance to cutting, with all the ambiguity that this technique brings.[14]

It was certainly necessary to get rid of text in order to explore the capacity for abstraction in the image and editing.

However, there are still forty minutes of dialogue in the film, and forty minutes is a lot. Where do these dialogues occur, and what are they about?

2001, Decentred Cinema

'Eighteen months ago, the first evidence of intelligent life off the earth was discovered. It was buried forty feet below the lunar surface, near the crater Tycho. Except for a single, very powerful radio emission aimed at Jupiter, the four-million-year-old black monolith has remained completely inert, its origin and purpose still a total mystery.' Thus goes the end of Floyd's prerecorded video briefing that plays once Hal has been disconnected. I quote it because these are the last words spoken in the film, before the film launches wholeheartedly into the non-verbal audiovisual trip (aside from the title 'Jupiter and Beyond the Infinite'). Floyd's words are the most explicit thing we hear about the mystery around which the film swirls incessantly, and the enigmas it constructs. 'I don't like to talk about *2001* much,' Kubrick remarked when the film came out, 'because it's essentially a non-verbal experience. ... It attempts to communicate more to the subconscious and to the feelings than it does to the intellect.'[15]

As we have already noted, only the central sections – the Floyd mission and the Discovery episode – include dialogue scenes, but many of the things said therein are said in order to conceal (for diegetic reasons already examined). The dialogues where the characters have no reason to hide anything, such as personal telephone conversations, appear conventional and uninteresting. This owes less to their actual content, which is sincere and without pretence, than to the way they are shown: from a distance (the voices as well as the faces), and always from a single perspective – the viewpoint of someone who is getting the message but is, in a way, already elsewhere.

Finally, the intentional discrepancy between the futurism of the situations on the one hand – the immensity of the cosmic setting for the characters – and, on the other, the very ordinariness of the dialogues, gives the latter a shade of insignificance. The rarity and apparent secondary status of the dialogue do not allow us, however, to consider *2001* as being like a silent film.

In the silent era, with very few exceptions, not only did films have dialogue, indicated in intertitles (when they were not conveyed by moving lips in the images), but there was also a narrative text, conveyed by the same means. Narrating title cards did not just present the characters and the setting; they could also indicate what was going on inside the head of a character, pass judgments, state the moral of the story ... all the while pretending to let the images 'speak for themselves'. Here we have an early form of this duplicity upon which the cinema is constructed, saying and telling while seemingly only showing.[16]

But what Kubrick tried to do in some scenes of *2001* – present dialogues that are decentred from what occupies the spectator's mind – could not have been done outside the context of sound cinema. Try to transpose into silent film a couple of scenes where a character asks someone, 'Did you have a good trip?' (when Floyd arrives) or 'A little coffee?' (in the shuttle going to the crater). Instead of being heard, these lines would appear on title cards, and thus would necessarily become the centre of the images they appear with. The fact that in the universe of the sound film they are *superimposed* on other sounds and on to images that draw our attention towards other things gives them different weight and meaning. Kubrick's cinema here employs what I call *decentred dialogue*, where we feel that the world 'is not reduced to the function of embodying dialogue'.[17]

Furthermore, in certain scenes of *2001*, speech seems to make the action stop and the camera freeze. During his presidency it was said that it was hard for Gerald Ford to walk and chew gum at the same time. This remark reverberates in the heroes of *2001*: they do not do anything when they speak, and do not speak while walking or doing something. Which is normally not considered too good a way to construct a scene.

Just as in *2001* there is no interweaving of speech and action[18] – the very interweaving that the classical cinema deploys constantly to tie together the various elements – so dialogue lines themselves rarely overlap. Whether in a banal conversation or a crucial dialogue scene such as the one pitting Hal and Dave against each other, each character says strictly what he has to say, and only when it is his turn. It is as if each line uttered is punctuated by an 'over' before another character replies. This formal ping-ponging of speech is underscored by a sort of passive impassibility on the part of the camera; it seems to formally note each thing said. We find the same tendency in the briefing and interview scenes in *The Shining* (the beginning) and *Full Metal Jacket*.

By refusing the interweaving, by removing from his film the play of echoes and reciprocal punctuation that makes image and dialogue (and more generally the shown and the said) support and guarantee one another, Kubrick strips the sound film bare, decentres it.

The closer the cinema moves in the direction of such stripping or reduction, but retains the usual ingredients of speech, action and editing, the more acutely it encounters the contradictions. Why is a particular section of dialogue not dramatised? Why not use images exclusively? And what does a certain shot transition signify?

The strength of Kubrick's film lies in having kept alive all the contradictions of his project, retaining dialogue, character and narrative form, while still making an experimental work. We might also say that in fact he had no choice, and that the conditions of production, as well as the commercial success he sought, all prevented him from moving towards abstract film. Little matter – for we can just as well say that his choice to remain in the vein of popular cinema while reinvigorating it is also an auteur's choice, not a limitation or constraint; and that he chose contradiction.

It is a misunderstanding to see the cinema as entirely an art of the image. Film is also an art of movement, an art of space, an art of editing, an art of recorded speech and acting, an audiovisual art, and these elements can enter into contradiction with one another. There is really no reason why seeing should come to the aid of what we hear, nor why listening should help what we see, nor why movement should not disrupt compositional lines,[19] in that these elements influence each other, combine with each other and are even at odds with each other.

In *2001*, speeches are interrupted as if to help us see, and action is frozen as if to help us hear. In combination with the film's many ellipses and scarcity of dialogue, this dissociation of elements had unexpected effects on the film's first audiences. One example of the effect of dissociating word and image: on hearing Floyd tell the Russians that he is going 'to Clavius', many spectators thought that he was going to a planet named Clavius. 'Why they think there's a planet Clavius I'll never know,' commented Kubrick. 'But they hear him being asked, "Where are you going?" and he says, "I'm going to Clavius." With many people – boom – that one word registers in their heads and they don't look at fifteen shots of the moon, they don't see he's going to the moon.'[20]

It is true that the word 'moon' is pronounced only once in the dialogue, when Floyd has to state his identity and destination for the voiceprint security system before boarding his flight. Quite naturally, the Russians and Floyd just refer to their respective stations by name: Chalinko, Clavius. Seeing the moon and hearing the word 'moon' are very different things, and since in the film the word and the image are dissociated in time, a sort of schizophrenia results, which goes far beyond the question of any laziness or ignorance on the part of the audience.

Words Give Voice to the World's Emptiness or Fullness[21]

Many people apprehended *2001* as the most cinematic of films, in that it borrows from no external code or genre and speaks a pure language of cinema. It 'signifies itself' as music seemingly does, according to a frequently invoked claim.[22]

This seems to me too beautiful to be true. It is easy to say that since the characters never utter such fateful words as *extraterrestrial*, since they do not articulate what is happening and no one exclaims 'Good God, a monolith', then the film is avoiding recourse to this 'extrinsic' element that is speech (according to conceptions that continue to prevail). For at the same time, the film imposes subtitles pregnant with meaning, and stamps them on to what we see and hear. These are as radical a forcing of meaning as any dialogue. In what is literally only the story of a band of apes in prehistoric times, for example, the subtitle 'The Dawn of Man' urges the spectator to read much more.

As for the justly admired sequence of Hal's murder of the three hibernating astronauts, a sequence Mario Falsetto analyses as an example of pure cinema on the basis of its absence of dialogue and the way it uses editing as its sole means of signification, you still have to admit that it would be incomprehensible were it not for the use of text – the series of messages flashing on the control monitors. Text means recourse to the verbal, and in a sense these messages on the screen could just as well be replaced (as they are in later science-fiction films like *The Andromeda Strain* and *Alien*) by prerecorded spoken warnings: instead of reading 'Computer malfunction' and then 'Life functions critical' and finally 'Life functions terminated', we would hear it, spoken perhaps by a female voice. So here we definitely have the audiovisual with language, the only difference being that this text is read rather than heard. Kubrick's audacity lies not in economising on the verbal, but in using text as a discontinuous and partial element in a system of discontinuities. What happens, happens between the shots and between the monitors, but also, crucially, between the texts conveyed on the monitors: between, for example, 'Life functions critical' and 'Life functions terminated'. The before and after of different shots, but also the before and after of two instances of text.

In passing, let us appreciate in these messages on the monitor two kinds of prophetic humour. There is the humour that consists in using an apparent euphemism so as not to say 'death'. But medical progress has given us good reason to use euphemisms: cardiac death no longer sufficing to define the state of cessation of life, what criterion is viable that will not be revised in its turn some day? The other joke is the use of one word, *function*, to designate (and thus place on the same level) both the activity of the computer and the normal processes of human life reduced to the physiological. In terms of narrative logic, we realise that the builders of the Discovery must have had a good sense of black humour and also plenty of cynicism, since they already planned for, made and installed the warning message 'Life functions terminated', designed to flash calmly like other messages. Nor did they take the trouble to personalise it; the same message suffices for all three cosmonauts, who die collectively and anonymously, as if the idea of an incident affecting a single one of the three in hibernation was thrown out in advance.

Let us imagine that the name of each of them (a modest label on each coffin, as for a package, but rendered hardly readable for the spectator) were to be highlighted on the monitor. This would yield an altogether different scene, and we would be witnessing three individualised deaths. The way in which it is stated – here, the way it is written, omitting the identity of the victims – remains crucial. This is a far cry from a cinema of 'pure' images and sounds, despite what a narrow interpretation – the frequent characterisation of *2001* as a non-verbal experience – would have us think. The non-verbal is itself actually a category of the verbal (negation itself is a symbolic, linguistic act – think of its role in mathematics – and the possibility of negating is a condition of language and thus its confirmation). It is thus not in Kubrick – who had been a creator of photos that were to resonate together with captions in magazines, and who then became skilled in his films in using the voice-over, another linguistic effect – that we shall encounter the naïve idealism that consists in believing that the non-verbal, as absolute, is achieved in cinema solely through the suppression of words.[23]

The dialogues in *2001* rarely concern what everyone is thinking about, that is, the existence of another life form in the universe; the lines are deliv-

ered by the actors without drama; and they are superficial in their politeness and bureaucratic neutrality. But these factors do not make the
dialogue unimportant. This would be like saying that in a dissonant chord,
the most significantly dissonant note does not count.[24]

What the film opposes to the smooth and impenetrable surface (the
monolith) are these words whose banality rebounds from it. If there were
not these words to 'ring' off it, we would not experience its diamond-hard
resistance.

The film inhabits this very divergence between the said and the shown.
But the said is here something quite different from the way to highlight
the shown. It remains – above and beyond its content – the only way to
give voice to the emptiness or the fullness of the world.

We can describe the cinema as an art where the confrontation of the said
and the shown manifests itself in a completely new way.[25]

I call *said* all that passes through the medium of language (in the strict
sense of the word), whether by the auditory channel (dialogue, spoken narration, song lyrics when they occur), or by the visual channel (subtitles,
intertitles, written/printed text within the image); the *shown* is what we are
given to perceive as a visible or auditory thing. The shown should not be
confused with the visible, and can be auditory as well as visual. Sound
effects or noises, the timbre of actors' voices, independent of the content
of what they say, are examples of 'shown' sound elements.

2001 is exemplary for its dialectical play between the said and the shown.
Much of the film consists of the shown, but it manages to inscribe the
shown within the not-said – and how can you create a shown and a not-
said if not through a said?

But also, it is through an open confrontation of the said with the image
and with the *face* that we can truly measure and affirm the power of lies.[26]

The Power of Lies

When Hal declares he knows that someone is trying to disconnect him and
Dave answers, 'I don't know what you're talking about, Hal,' we feel
strangely ashamed. Dave has good reason not to tell the truth to a dangerous enemy, of course. But he does it in front of us, and at that moment
the reflections of control panel lights that flash rhythmically on his face

bring out his features and his eyes, and seem to make a display of the fact that he is lying.

The characters at this point are diegetically *connected by voice*, but in filmic space they are *connected through vision*, via editing. The shot–reverse shot exists only on the screen and through the mediation of our gaze, since nothing establishes that Dave sees Hal's eye at that moment, nor Hal the face of Dave. Both are looking at us, and look at each other only through us. We are witnesses as much as we are relays for this lie.

Do not forget that Hal has also lied by saying nothing of what he knows about the mission's goal; the scene in which he interrogates Dave consists of dissembling, and retroactively turns us into witnesses of a lie of omission. But we cannot spot the slightest trace of this lie on the teller's non-existent face.

It should be clear that *2001* implicates us inextricably in the guilt of the gaze addressed to the camera. It is the gaze of the triumphant lie.

All the human characters of *2001* have a good reason not to give themselves away. Heywood Floyd has to keep the secret of the monolith discovery from the crew at first, during what is supposed to be a routine trip, and again in the interrogation to which the Soviet representative suavely subjects him. Then Bowman and Poole are constantly under the eye and ear of Hal, whom they are watching in turn.

The smoothness and polish Kubrick gives to the film, wherein the opaque monolith and the equally opaque actors square off, bears comparison to a chess or poker game (Kubrick was an avid poker player) – and also to lying.

The impenetrable quality of the image and the film is akin to the child's discovery of the power of lying when it realises that Pinocchio's nose belongs to the world of fiction; in other words, a well-told lie *cannot* be seen.

The child has an overwhelming and sacred experience when for the first time he is brought to lie to someone's face. Anyone who has never done it would not be completely human. How else could we feel the nobility and the stakes of language, how else could we know the price of truth?

It is thus in the very experience where it seems to profane and betray language that we consecrate it; and *2001* magnifies the shameful exaltation of this experience.

Interpretations of a Monolith

How easy it would be to sidestep the task of understanding *2001*, to live in bliss refusing any effort to find meaning in it beyond what we see and hear at each moment. If this were all there were to it, the work in all its beauty would be little other than a machine to turn on, so to speak, to stimulate the desire for meaning even as it bypasses the law of the signifier.

It is not by accident that I have written 'in bliss', as the film devotes itself largely to the satisfaction of needs, in the way we imagine a newborn baby who has just had its fill. Like Floyd, who sleeps calmly on his flight towards the lunar station while a stewardess sees to his comfort; like Bowman, who finds himself at the end of the film in a four-star hotel suite where he is fed and housed to the end of his days, we can let ourselves be carried away at particular moments (the 'Blue Danube' sequences, for example) by turning and spinning shapes and by music that does anything but disturb; we have only to yield.

At the same time, the most famous shot transition of the film and perhaps in all of cinema, the cut from the bone to the heavens full of flying vehicles, requires an effort of *interpretation* on the part of the laziest spectator in order to make any narrative sense. It requires that we establish a relationship of some kind between these two shots and their content, via abstract thinking that can perceive the form shared by each object. Beyond that, each person is free not to see a causal relationship between the flying bone and the spaceships. But the spectator will have nevertheless made a minimal logical connection consisting (even in negative form) in perceiving the resemblance between the bone and the vehicle, and to draw a connection, a relation not only of analogy, but also of cause and effect, a 'rhyme'. S/he will make the same leap of abstraction that the apeman makes in inventing the tool.

This edit is the very act of abstraction, since it constitutes a definitive, irrevocable leap into language, into the symbolic.

Because of the edit, but without the edit stating it explicitly or completely, we decide that this object is a tool, a weapon, the beginning of everything man will invent, much in the same way that we decide in chess that one parallelepedic form is a rook, and another smaller one is a pawn.

People Stop Talking

2001 highlights the problem of interpretation, if for no other reason than because the characters encounter this problem in the monolith they discover. But if the monolith has the quality of a closed book, *2001* itself is both a closed book, since it dissembles its explicit meaning, and an open book since it makes a display of its literal content, even its gaps and ellipses and the 'symbolic' (and irreducible) edits it contains.

Kubrick's film, through brilliant ellipses as well as arbitrary superimpositions of music and image, is a veritable interpretory labyrinth, a machine to set spectators' interpretation glands salivating.

We could be happy just contemplating the forms, but that is impossible. We must understand, hence we project. The film holds up a mirror to our perpetual temptation to project. In this mirror, we see ourselves madly constructing intentions and meaning – and being unable to support the idea that things are not what they are.

Besides, what is it that an image 'is'? Presented a face in close-up, can we consider it as it is, in other words, not expressing anything in particular if that happens to be the case?

In reality we are unable to allow images their opacity; we are compelled to judge.

For example, Dave and Frank seem cold or lacklustre to us, but we forget they exist in a situation of constant surveillance, and that if Heywood Floyd is politely reserved, it is in a world of opposing superpowers where everybody has to be wary of everyone else.

We also have no reason to doubt Floyd's sincere affection for his family, especially his daughter. Nor Frank's love for his parents when he sees them wish him happy birthday in the recorded message; if he has an inscrutable look, it is because he has dark glasses on, and since he is alone and his parents are not seeing him, he has no particular reason to smile.

Coldness is therefore yet another interpretation that the film allows us to project on to what we see. *2001* highlights the cinema as an art of 'allowing'; based on given textual elements, viewers are left to project interpretations on to concretely irreducible things. When the computer itself says to Dave, 'Perhaps I'm projecting my own concern about it,' it is alluding to this process.

The film has two emblematic shots shots that face off, in a way. One shows the monolith among the apes; the other, the space pod in the period bedroom. It is impossible to only see them literally. Each presents an incongruous object, from another era and an other space than where it appears, and which cries out for interpretation. This is a plea that the characters could never answer, and for good reason: they are pre-human apes in one case and an astronaut stricken with mutism in the other.

In the film, *people stop talking in the presence of the monolith*. Even the astronauts of Clavius fall silent just as they discover it and snap photos in front of it. It is doubtless for this reason that outside the film, and in books or essays like this, we make up for it with so many words.

Interpretations: from Numerology to Alchemy

Beginning even with its title, *2001* lends itself to all manner of *numerological* speculations, like those that Carolyn Geduld advanced regarding the number '4'. As soon as you state that the film is divided into four movements (we have already said that this is certainly not the only possible way of seeing it), and that the monolith appears four times, and that the title has four digits and a film screen has four sides, you start to see fours everywhere. Of course, you can take any number and apply it to a film or literary work and, with enough intellectual gymnastics, you will always come up with something. In *War and Peace* Tolstoy demonstrates with gusto the indiscriminate character of such speculations. The character Pierre Bezukhov convinces himself through numerologic calculations not only that Napoleon is the Beast of the Apocalypse, whose number is 666, but that he himself is the man chosen to destroy him.

The *alchemical* interpretive framework has also been developed, particularly in an article by Jean-Marc Elsholz.[27] The symbolic and chemical forms in *2001* certainly lend themselves to this approach, and Bowman (the archer) who is reborn out of himself, in a bed of 'matrimonial proportions', may call the androgyne Rebis to mind. Equally tempting is *formal symbolism*: the sphere (of the stars, and the pods) and the parallelepiped (of the monolith, and associated with the rectangle enclosing Hal's eye) are the most prominent forms. Claude-Alexis Gras invites us to note that the triangle is absent, even though suggested.[28]

I have nothing against such interpretations in principle, but what sometimes bothers me is the way they are often carried out, when they reduce
the work to what they set out to demonstrate in the first place. Other
studies seem aware of the arbitrary, contingent and contradictory aspects
of all works of nature or of human endeavour, and do not try to reduce
them. These are the ones that interest me, shedding light on the work and
bringing out its contours, rather than merely treating it as an encrypted
message that will become transparent once 'decoded'.

To interpret *2001* as some sort of hidden message to be read along a
single axis is to distort the fact that the film is directly about interpretation
itself. This is true not simply on the level of content, but in its cinematic
language – shot transitions, editing, framing.

The Head of the Camera

A large part of *2001* imperturbably connects its narrative parts together in
the spirit of Tolstoy: static shots are linked with other static shots, achiev-
ing a sort of flattening of objects and events. Characters in these shots are
often looking at screens; or we see them from the back and their facial
expression is not visible; or we see them frontally and their face shows
nothing.

We also find many close-ups of Dave (but almost not a single one of
Floyd). The close-up, when associated with a complementary cue that may
be auditory or visual, is often used to designate that something is happening in the character's head. Here, inside Dave, it seems to say that nothing
is there ...

It is with this nothing that we need to begin again.

An effect of a specifically cinematic nature arises from the confrontation
between the *insistence of the camera's gaze* brought to an object, conveyed
by a close-up of the object or by the camera's prolonged immobility, and
the *'indifference' of this object of the gaze* to this interest shown, to this insistence. If a film shows me object or character X and lingers on it for a long
time, X must be important, but it remains unreadable and immobile. The
narration designates X to me, but what is X thinking and seeing, this X that
is thus designated and also the designating authority?

The insistence-on-showing in the cinema (this sense, hypersignified in

Kubrick, may be created by different means – slowness of rhythm, sharpness and brightness of the image, clarity of framing) creates a paradoxical effect. It seems to show things as they are and invite us to accept them thus; and at the same time it designates itself as a finger insistently pointing at things. The object of the camera's look is thus doubled and split – and our relation to it altered – by the insistence on showing it and making it occupy a certain duration in the film.

By its nature (in contrast to, say, painting) the cinema does double duty, since it utilises duration, a duration it itself imposes, as a means subtly to do something other than which it claims to be doing. If a camera remains fixed on a setting once the actors have left the frame – a technique Losey uses several times in *Accident*, for example – it is impossible for us not to see an intention, even as we sense that this empty setting does not care in the least. The opaqueness of the setting is redoubled by a second opaqueness that we might put this way: what is happening right now *in the head of the camera*?

Alignments[29]

Let us imagine three objects – for example, three pebbles in a landscape – aligned by chance, 'chance' being an inextricable intersection of causes along several axes of time. Immediately we would seek an intentionality that would explain the pattern. Similarly, man created constellations by associating some stars with others, stars that have no inherent connection but are lined in a row when seen from the earth.

> The idea of a magical alignment of the sun, the earth, and the moon, or of Jupiter and its moons, was used throughout the film to represent something magical and important about to happen. I suppose the idea had something to do with the strange sensation one has when the alignment of the sun takes place at Stonehenge.[30]

Kubrick thus uses this trope to awaken in us the idea of intentionality, but also of imminence. Alignment in astrology is a crossroads of trajectories recurring at well-determined intervals (like the alignment of a clock's hands at midnight). In much the same way, the director presents to us successions of shots on the linear axis of time as alignments with obvious intentionality, but also impenetrable, to a greater or lesser extent, and marked by the idea of before and after.

In Kubrick, at least in *2001*, the image is very often before the important and decisive event, and sometimes after, but it is rarely during.[31]

Are there few shots of 'during'?

Ambivalence Embodied: Rhymes

Let us call rhymes the typically cinematic echoes among situations, repeated elements given to us without always being explicitly designated as such, resonating between themselves and leaving us the choice of whether to group them together. Though rarely satisfying our thirst or immediate comprehension, *2001* invites us to find rhymes everywhere because of its mysteriousness and aspects of its structure.

I am not limiting rhymes to repetitions of situations, such as the repetition of a birthday scene, or meals (apes, Floyd, cosmonauts, Dave and Frank in the *Discovery*, Dave eating alone at the end), or sleep (apes 'sleeping badly', Floyd sleeping like a baby, Hunter, Kimball and Kaminsky in hibernation, Frank and Dave sleeping in shifts, Dave dying and being reborn in a bed). A rhyme can also be a concrete element, directly cinematic, that concerns the slightest thing. Its use is not specific to Kubrick by any means, but the very conception of *2001* and its subject give it a central place.

The rhyming return of a silent gesture – the hesitant drawing of a hand towards a smooth wall – when we see an ape do it or a cosmonaut four million years later, is an overwhelming and almost sacred 'non-verbal experience' as only the cinema can offer. To be meaningful, a rhyme requires that the cosmonaut had never seen or imagined the ape's gesture. Amnesia, or non-consciousness, is a condition for rhyme.

Other prominent rhymes in *2001* are:

• The edited graphic match as rhyme: a bone, an elongated space vehicle;
• Alignments of objects in space, in the beginning and at the end;
• Shots involving an incongruously inserted object: the monolith among the apes, the pod in the period bedroom suite.

We can also find rhymes made from oppositions: the ape brandishes his weapon in triumph, while the future-man's arm floats as it abandons his pen in space.

The craziest rhymes are possible: the Rodin-like thinking pose, the hand near the mouth: we see Floyd this way as he plays chess, and then Poole as he encounters the byzantine instructions for the toilet in weightless space.

The tapir skull crushed by the ape and Dave's glass that is crushed by gravity from its fall: should we consider this a rhyme? Or only a distant echo?

And finally here is a rhyme I find myself especially drawn to, but which like many others is impossible to document without rerunning the film: I see internal rhymes whenever something turns around on its axis. What could be more cinematic than an image of someone turning her head, turning his eyes or entirely turning around, as in the 'eternalised' shot in *Titanic*?[32]

This is what the pod that turns against Poole does, and this moment has been carefully prepared to surprise us – since up to that point the sphere turned only under Dave's vocal command.

And what another pod later does too, this time a pod piloted by Dave who, having had to leave Poole's body out in space, goes back to the Discovery to confront Hal with pincers extended, with a very theatrical look – 'draw!' like Sergio Leone's Westerns (which influenced 60s cinema, in my opinion).

We even have, here, rhyming scenes: Frank's sortie is almost identical to Dave's and seems to repeat the same shots: the same sounds of breathing (possibly a bit faster) and the same parallel editing. Only Frank's spacesuit is yellow, in contrast to Dave's red one.

The pod that kills Frank under Hal's remote command, and the pod that Dave manoeuvres to grasp the body of Frank, taking it in its arms like a futuristic Pietà, have an identical appearance. The gesture for killing and the gesture of embracing are the same. This idea is taken up again in Ridley Scott's *Alien*, where the monster stretches out its arms to those it is about to kill.

Rhyme in this sense is ambivalence embodied in a gesture or an object.

The pod Dave manoeuvres turns twice. Once landed in the period room, Dave turns twice towards an other who each time is himself – first an astronaut with his helmet, turning toward, a noise that draws him; second, an old man in a robe, turning toward, someone who is ... the camera. Like the mother of Norman Bates at the end of Hitchcock's *Psycho*, but very slowly.

Finally, the Star Child of the final image turns slowly towards us, as if asymptotically, since a fade-out prevents us from seeing it look directly at us.

Remember that *A Clockwork Orange* takes up where *2001* leaves off, via the frank look into the camera, in this case Malcolm McDowell's, full of defiance.

The Monolith as Discontinuity

But the principal object of rhyming (ultimately reduced to just that) is the monolith itself. This monolith, in the wild adventure of *2001*, 'worked' well, if by worked we mean solicited all possible interpretations and exceeded them. The monolith cries out for interpretation; we might say that that is what it is there for, it is built into the filmic system.

1. The monolith is an anthropological symbol. It refers to many ancient monuments erected in stone – Stonehenge, for example – monuments located in several parts of the world, and whose function scientists continue to puzzle about, especially when it is claimed that they are related to astronomical alignments. Even if we do not view them as the proof of God or extraterrestrial beings (as innumerable occultist speculations do), they captivate the imagination with the stubborn muteness of their presence.

   In *2001* the monolith always appears as a single object. But since it returns at different times with similar traits (the sun hitting it, a brutally abrupt interruption following it), it is as if it forms an *alignment with itself* through time.

2. In its form and its verticality, it is a totem, a phallic symbol of energy, an object of adoration. It is the symbolic phallus in the psychoanalytical sense, that is, the symbol of the 'sovereign good'.[33]

3. The monolith is a symbol of burial: one of the rare things we find out about the one found on the moon is that it was 'deliberately buried'. It is exhumed as if it were some sort of pharaonic sarcophagus. This refers back to funerary symbolism, which has a strong presence in the film.

One of the first signs shown to us in the beginning is the blanched skeleton of an anthropoid ape, left where it died; this tells us, essentially, that we are in an era before man. Much later, when the three astronauts in deep freeze move directly from hibernation to death in their containers, they do so with absolutely no ceremony paid them. The sole survivor, Dave Bowman, in order to stay alive himself, is forced to send the body of the dead Frank into the interstellar void without even a ritual word, although it had been his natural, pious, human impulse to recover the body. (The theme of what the burial rite might become in space and in the future hovers over much modern science fiction; see, for example, the *Alien* series.)[34]

Finally, what embodies the authority of memory and of the monument at the same time, is the monolith. But curiously this monolith is virgin, this Tablet of the Law without commandments, this stele with no inscriptions, rigorously identical across millions of years – we could even say it is an anti-monument, an apparent negator of history that, on the other hand, its presence seems to have set in motion.

4. It is a signifier of abstraction itself. It appears as 'the same' in different instances and in different scales, horizontal or vertical.

It is also symbolic of the *movement* of abstraction. In its unassimilable nature, indissoluble in the forms that surround it, the monolith can very well be seen as a mathematical symbol of relation unifying disparate objects of the world, and inviting us to consider them from an abstract point of view. It is the letter or the number.

When seen by characters (it is seen and not-seen, present and no-longer-there), the monolith is always vertical. When not necessarily seen by a character, at the end of the film, it is horizontal.

In its status as a geometrical object immediately prone to be abstracted, repeated, echoed through the course of time, the monolith-object itself accedes from the outset to the status of a mental image.

5. Because of its muteness, the monolith is also an analyst, a 'subject assumed to know'![35] While Hal speaks (to the point of taking himself for a subject), the monolith remains silent.

The monolith is actually the opposite of Hal, the computer whose auditory and visual embodiment is limited for us to one eye (always the same, wherever it is) and one voice. In short, he is a very present character, but we still cannot cross-check things he says with what is in his eyes (for the eye is without a look) or his gestures or his facial expressions. The film never even shows us Hal's circuits functioning. If he exists for us, it is because he speaks, and says things like, 'My mind is going. I can feel it. There is no question about it.'

Hal and the monolith: an invisible protagonist that speaks and a visible protagonist that does not. The two figures do not cross paths in the film, this talking computer and this mute extraterrestrial artefact; this is what the two have in common, they are the counter-rhymes (rhyme by contrast) of each other.[36]

6. The monolith also exists in time as being there, then 'no longer there', and the discontinuity of its presence refers to what Lacan calls the child's 'games of occultation', first discussed by Freud in *Beyond the Pleasure Principle*.[37] These games consist of playing on appearances and disappearances mastered by the voice, such as 'peekaboo', and are the foundation of the symbolic, of language as 'murder of the thing'.

Similarly, the monolith in the film is characterised by being there and then not there, then there again. Its first two appearances are marked by a brutal interruption/commutation on both visual and audio tracks. The monolith slices into time – it cuts time, as it cuts space (by its form and verticality), and in this sense it is the letter itself, beyond interpretation.

While Hal is on the side of the maternal and continuous, the monolith is thus the Father, as discontinuity.[38]

Epilogue: a Room too Large

We must finally return to childhood – which is where *2001* ends, and also which is that cradle of comfort and trust where we first see Floyd, at the beginning of the human story.

Just as the Orion is too large for the sleeping Floyd when he is its sole passenger, so at the end, the room and the bed are too big for Dave alone.

Dumont and Monod are right to speak of the 'astral foetus', and let us not forget that the foetus presupposes (at least in symbolic terms) a placenta and maternal bosom to contain and nurture it. The presence of the foetus 'mamma-ises' the universe, associates it with maternal security (to borrow a formulation from Françoise Dolto), and suggests that the interplanetary void can be an environment that is protective rather than hostile.[39]

The spirit of childhood has long been part of Kubrick's universe, even with the character of Lolita, who is by no means reduced to the role of a sex object. The unfocused, unfinished aspect of the face of Ryan O'Neal in *Barry Lyndon* is another example, as is the way Kubrick brought out the infantile side of George C. Scott in *Dr Strangelove* as a nervous muncher of peanuts.

In Kubrick's work the child is often single and solitary. Heywood's daughter is an only child whom he affectionately calls Squirt and who appears spoiled. Lolita is an only child, as is Alex in *A Clockwork Orange*, and little Danny in *The Shining* as well.

This solitariness of the child lends a closeness and pathos to the mother–son couple, in Lady Lyndon and her son in *Barry Lyndon*, and Wendy and Danny in the labyrinth of *The Shining*.

In Kubrick's hands, between Hal and the monolith, we are really not that far removed from mummy and daddy. Like *A Clockwork Orange*'s Alex, who is an ultraviolent psychopath but drinks milk and lives at home, the environment where Dave is ultimately 'housed' is a nurturing one, taking up where the one maintained by Hal left off.

Food in the infantile, elementary sense plays an important role, as we see in many of Kubrick's films, where it refers to the relieving of anxiety. We have only to look at the insistence on this idea in *The Shining* and its abundance of food reserves, and the description of the Overlook Hotel as a vast pantry. There is the comic scene in *Dr Strangelove* about the American military survival kit, and the pie-throwing battle (eventually cut from the film). And let us not forget the first shot in *A Clockwork Orange* with Alex drinking his enriched milk, nor that the first part of *Full Metal Jacket* is predicated on the bulimia of one of the soldiers, nor that the first shot of Danny in *The Shining* shows him eating.

Finally, the scene of Poole's birthday focuses on a virtual cake, a transmitted image; his parents show it to him but of course Poole cannot eat it. This scene is more heart-rending than derisory. The parents are real and sincere in their simplicity – it is the context that makes them look touchingly small with the cake. But you cannot eat an image.

2001 claims to be descended from the *Odyssey*, which itself has more to do with food than is normally thought.

2001 and Universal Myths

A 'space odyssey', says the original title. Does the film's relationship to the epic poem attributed to Homer and long considered the model of travel and adventure stories rise above cliché?

In Homer, all Odysseus wants is to return to the fold of his little kingdom of Ithaca, which he evokes in moving terms. Michel Serres has persuasively argued that Odysseus is the anti-adventurer, not at all interested in the customs and natural wonders his adventures lead him to discover. Odysseus's voyage is a *nostos* – a Greek word meaning return and the root of 'nostalgia', and a word intimately connected to the entire branch of mythology that recounts the exploits of the Greek heroes returning after the Trojan War.

In the opposing camp, it seems, Dave Bowman is a man without attachments, the least rooted of all the film's characters, since, as Michel Ciment pointed out, we see neither his daughter (as we see Floyd's) nor his parents (as we see Poole's). But at the film's end, Kubrick lands him in a sort of artificial Ithaca (unless perhaps it is a grotto of Calypso) where there is never a care about food and drink: the period bedroom. In this sense, 2001 harks to the Homeric tradition, which does not hesitate to devote as many lines to the pleasures of the good life as it does to the exploits. This is one thing that lends credibility to the revolutionary hypothesis that the *Odyssey* was the work of a woman.

Homer's Odysseus is buffeted from shore to shore by the winds of fate, but also often taken in and pampered by various protectors, including the goddess Athena. Bowman goes from the initially protective hands of Hal – to whom the first version of the screenplay gave the name of the Greek goddess – to those of invisible entities who are benevolent, if not indifferent.

It is quite evident that the *Odyssey* was an inspiration for the story, but an inspiration only. Certainly, Dave finds himself alone, just as Odysseus loses all his companions, but while in Homer the gods Athena and Poseidon embody rival protective and persecuting forces, for Dave the two are blended into the single figure of Hal.[40]

Nevertheless, the relation to time in the first part of the film evokes in an unsettling way a family of tales like the *Odyssey* that circulate in various forms around the world, and in which a simple human (Rip van Winkle, Urashima Taro) is plucked out of time by a divinity who shares with him the delights of the life of the immortals. This type of story has found an extraordinary kind of validation in theories of relativity and on the connection between space and time. Theoretically, a man who travelled through space at phenomenal speed and then returned to earth would age less quickly than the people he would return to.

In the traditional Japanese tale, the fisherman Urashima Taro lives in a realm of pleasure with a goddess (like Odysseus and Calypso); but he wishes to go back to visit his parents, after which he promises to return. This causes the goddess great sadness; she gives him a pouch with a strict warning not to open it. When the fisherman gets to his village, it is completely transformed, and he realises that he has been gone for several centuries. He breaks his pledge and opens the pouch, from which there escapes a sort of wind. All at once the spell that kept him outside ordinary time is broken, and his body grows old and disintegrates.

The plot of *2001* removes a good number of men from the course of normal time. There are the astronauts Kaminsky, Hunter and Kimball; and they die in a few seconds. And through the magic spell of editing, Kubrick takes Dave Bowman through several decades in three minutes. The three minutes and three edits suggest two contradictory things: both a vast span of diegetic time, and, through editing, the materialisation of accelerated ageing in film time. To top it all, the historical discrepancy between the period decor and the astronaut costume elicits a veritable temporal vertigo.

Ageing through the discovery of one's image in the mirror.

Through which we once again return to head-on confrontation and aggression.

The Beast that Cannot Be Denied

In *2001*, the first jubilation is also destruction. This jubilation seems to surpass the 'utilitarian' character of discovering a new way to obtain food. Needlessly destroying a skull seems to be an end in itself.

We cannot avoid imagining that Kubrick's work inspires questionable passions if we see it as singing the praises of an amoral desire for power. Kubrick shows the joy of smashing things to pieces, of desecration, domination and winning – but he does so in order to tell us something about our species.

The theme of aggression 'in the mirror' in *2001* is established quickly at the outset by showing war between the same-species ape clans. Your worst enemies are those like you, the film seems to say; note that we never see combat between the apemen and their predators, nor any apemen hunting their own prey. The society of 2001, for its part, seems to have temporarily suspended warfare in favour of mutual surveillance. This society also relies on the sublimation of sports: there is a judo match on a TV screen on the shuttle to the moon, Poole shadow-boxes and we see games such as Hal and Frank's chess game.

2001 is a film about a world where all aggressive behaviour is everywhere suppressed, policed and erased, and where it coldly comes back to haunt us through Hal's madness.

The shot of the Discovery where the computer temporarily rules, and of the small spherical pod with Dave within, briefly makes visible this face-to-face confrontation that was previously impossible. Now we notice that the space vessels have eyes that stare, claws to grip with and mouths to crush with.

The smooth and insipid politeness that reigns in the world of the future needs only the slightest disturbance to crack and allow the howling beast to reappear, even if the howling is silent. Thus in humans, who aspired to the state of angels, the beast cannot be denied.

Rebirth

Nevertheless *2001* is, in spite of itself, an optimistic film. It is like a missile that was launched to be the most pessimistic film of Kubrick's career, even bleaker than the previous one, and which a strange fate then diverted from its target.

The spacecraft we see in the first image from the year 2001 were originally intended to be satellites crammed with nuclear weapons, weapons that the Star Child at the end was supposed to detonate. But as we know, the idea to make warheads of these objects was dropped, and the scene of a confrontation between the Star Child and the earth was also eliminated.

Perhaps we owe these last-minute changes to nothing more than Kubrick's concern not to repeat the horrible irony of *Dr Strangelove* – and, in a way, to a sort of gentility consisting of declining to pass us the same dish again at the dinner table.

At the same time, it seems to me that the very act of making *Dr Strangelove*, a film about nuclear destruction that could be useful and instructive as satire, was an act of fantastic optimism.

At any rate, after a film that ends with the end of the world, *2001* takes up at the start of the next century, and thus logically presents itself as a rebirth.

Dave, as I have said, has already experienced a rebirth when he makes his way back into the Discovery through the airlock. This moment of 'apnoea', where Dave musters all his forces and concentrates to hold his breath and go through a narrow passageway, strongly suggests childbirth, especially when we see the dramatic shot of the cosmonaut bathed in a red light. The shot begins in total silence, and then we hear a sort of liberating thunder when air surges in.

Then the 'child' is released into space, and discovers that the universe is for him a room too large. 'The most terrifying thing about the universe', said Kubrick, 'is not that it is hostile but that it is indifferent.'[41]

Kubrick confronts the frightening indifference of this large room that is the interstellar void, and he renders it in a deeply disturbing way (Poole's spacesuited body abandoned in space, until it is a speck that disappears in total darkness). But he attempts to transcend this terror and to bet on life.

2001 could be understood as a spiritualist film, but this would be to force its meaning: the film does not conclude anything. The extraterrestrials do not strike up contact; they bring no message of peace; they say nothing; they do not send Bowman back, reincarnated or otherwise, with a message that might be summarised in one word like love. (In this respect the sequel, *2010*, sentimentalised and limited the message of Kubrick's film.)

And yet, the Star Child is the promise that blossoms anew.

What is *2001* about? Well, it is about just what it seems to be about: life, the destiny of humanity, the human being as he experiences himself before the mystery of his existence, and the awareness of his ever-smaller place in the universe. Very simply, *2001* fills us with wonder because, in the face of the stars, it sings of the mystery of our life as humans.

Animals who know they will die, beings lost on earth, forever caught between two species, not animal enough, not cerebral enough.

Driven to discover the world, but seeing its boundaries retreat and its meaning diluted as we advance, like Dave we are brought back to the restricted space of the familiar.

Linguistic beings, but aware too that language engenders lies and betrays itself in the very gesture of its affirmation.

We are exalted at the idea that science makes us able to 'understand' the world and explain its laws, and to leave the bounds of our planet; but in the same movement we discover that by our nature we *project*, we cannot quite resign ourselves to the fact that language and meaning exist only in us, and are merely a kind of paint we use to colour the world.

In the major interview he did for *Playboy* in 1968, Kubrick spoke of his own 'awesome awareness of mortality' that prevented him from flying in aeroplanes (even though he had a pilot's licence). But he also described simply and beautifully the meaning life can have in a period that has proclaimed the death of God and, on the other hand, has yielded precise scientific data illustrating how small we are in relation to the grandeur of the universe. He recalled the spontaneous *joie de vivre* one sees in the existence of children. 'Children ... begin life with an untarnished sense of wonder, a capacity to experience total joy at something as simple as the greenness of a leaf.' A second stage brings the consciousness of death, decline and evil. But in a third stage, if the human being 'is reasonably strong – and lucky – he can emerge from this twilight of the soul into a rebirth of life's *élan*'. Though he can never again find 'the same pure sense of wonder' of his early years, 'he can shape something far more enduring and sustaining'.[42]

This is why Dave in the end is nothing more than an eye. No longer an eye for surveillance, since that was Hal's eye, nor an eye for sustaining lies, but rather an eye for contemplation, for being reborn out of the sense of wonder.

It seems to me, then, that far from any mythology of the superman (Dave's death and rebirth has nothing heroic about it), the end of *2001* can express the possibility of this rebirth anew, without limiting its meaning. Even though Kubrick as a director was quick to give expression to so many facets of scepticism and even pessimism, and could express so vividly the terror of death, such as in a moving sequence of *Paths of Glory*, he also tried to keep alive, to convey in a universal language with a vocabulary of marvellous imagery, a small leaf on a tree trembling in a holy wind, this 'pure sense of wonder' in which he recognised a sign of our human condition.

So there we are. I have no further arguments about *2001*. Each time I see it, this movie blows me away in every direction. We are like those apes facing the heavens, surrounded by the noises of the falling night.

Notes

1   [As explained in the previous chapter, Chion uses the word *commutation* idiosyncratically, to designate not only a substitution (its usual sense), but a switch, with the 'off-on' instantaneity of the light switch. *Commutateur* is the French word for an electric switch (as for a light). – Translator.]

2   Dumont and Monod, *Le Foetus astral*, p. 108.

3   In linguistics, these consist of the auditory traits that can vary in pronunciation of a word without the comprehension and identity of the word changing. In various regions and generations, there are several pronunciations of the letter 'a' in a word like 'man' that are not pertinent, in the sense that the word 'man' continues to be identified and understood as such. These are non-pertinent variations.

4   A transition often appears as an image that is 'called', invoked, magically, either by the aid of a character's line or a voice-over, or by the director's fiat.

5   The movie scene in front of which Floyd is sleeping aboard the Orion, showing a couple in a futuristic car, is all that *2001* shows us of earth at the time, which is to say, nothing.

6   Dumont and Monod discuss this with relevance and humour in their *Foetus astral* (pp. 53 ff). They even see in this phallic pen, 'put back in its place' by the stewardess, whom this 'divagation' is all about – a way of

signifying that the characters will do without women – the preparation of Bowman's final 'auto-fecundation' (ibid., p. 80).

   Often a rack-focus that puts the background into focus suggests sexual penetration or voyeurism. The stewardess is the sole image of a (possibly) unmarried adult woman. She is alone in the spaceship cabin with Floyd. The movie on the screen in front of Floyd shows a love story.

7 A Chinese proverb states that when someone points to the moon, the idiot looks at the finger. I think Kubrick wants us to look at both the moon and the finger, and he insists on the finger.

8 Philippe Pilard, *Barry Lyndon* (Paris: Nathan, Collection Synopsis, 1994).

9 Fellini describes the face as '*flou*' – blurred, soft, fuzzy, vague; Fellini was a great admirer of the film.

10 The history of art has represented nudity as a suit of armour, as a symbol connected with war (see, for example, Delacroix's *Liberty Leading the People*). My idea here is that an image magnified or foregrounded as such by its lighting, or its clarity, is less manipulable by other factors, such as sound.

11 Those of Hal are attributed to his *look*, those of the ape are attributable (with reservations) to his mind.

12 Dumont and Monod point out a poignant parallel: in the final sequence, 'the way the old man looks at the glass he has broken is reminiscent of the ape's look as he considers the bone before acquiring the intelligence to break it. They are both sitting; the sole difference is that the man has broken the glass by accident, while the ape looks at bones he will be breaking deliberately.' *Le Foetus astral*, p. 183.

13 In terms of the production history of the film, this insert shot is what it is – an exact duplicate of a shot viewed previously – solely because Kubrick apparently put it in at the last minute, and thus had no other choice but to use an existing shot. If he had had the opportunity to film the shot he wanted, perhaps he would have taken it from a different angle so as to avoid the repetition. However, nothing changes in terms of what this shot represents in Kubrick's *2001* as it exists.

14 The cut constantly erases itself in the meaning it creates. Its instantaneous moment has disappeared at the very moment its function has been fulfilled.

15 Quoted in Agel, p. 7.

16 See the work of Tom Gunning, André Gaudreault and Noël Burch on the 'primitive' narrative cinema and the dialectic between 'monstration' and 'narration'.

17 Chion, *Audio-vision: Sound on Screen,* pp. 182–3.

18 I use the term 'action' in a broad sense, including camera movements and zooms. The one exception to what is said above occurs in the conversation in the moon bus.

19 'Je hais le mouvement qui déplace les lignes' ('I hate movement which disturbs lines'), says Baudelaire in the sonnet 'La Beauté' ('Beauty').

20 Comments quoted by Jerome Agel, p. 102. Kubrick at least made sure his t's were crossed and his i's were dotted for the French dub of the film, where Floyd says, 'I'm going to Clavius, *our lunar station.*'

21 [This heading is Chion's poetic formulation. He explains that speech in a film is experienced as either resonating or not with the world in the film. On one level the French phrase he uses means that a sound such as tapping against a surface can indicate the spaces and volumes of a depicted world. But in further wordplay, Chion means that speech can indicate the presence or absence of resonance of *meaning* between the said and the shown. The world is 'full' where speech and world are in communication; man is not alone. It rings empty where there is no communication. – Translator.]

22 On this myth, see my book *La Musique au cinéma*, pp. 287ff.

23 In this connection, each of the deaths is presented in a different way. Frank's death is narrated through *mise en scène* (the body struggles, then floats in space) and through editing, but nothing and no one speaks about it. The death of the three astronauts is signified visually (the indicators of physiological activity on screen flatline) but also in writing, on the instrument panel. Hal's death is suggested visually (the red eye going out), but above all it is recounted orally ('My mind is going. I can feel it') by the voice of the party in question, with a coefficient of unreality and doubt. Finally, Dave's death occurs without written or spoken words, and opens on to what resembles a rebirth and a resurrection. None of the deaths is both shown and recounted.

24 For example, we might be tempted to say that in the scene in the

Orbiter Hilton, when the earth can be seen out of the window and yet characters exchange verbal banalities, the dialogue is unimportant. But what counts here is not the image in itself or the dialogue in itself, but the relationship, the distance, between the two: the dissonant interval.

25 On this subject see the chapter on Tarkovsky, 'Le Langage et le monde', in my book *La Toile trouée* (Paris: Cahiers du cinéma/Éditions de l'Étoile, 1988), pp. 169–74.

26 See the insightful remarks of Eric Rohmer, written in 1948, on lies in the cinema, reprinted on pages 32–3 of his collection entitled *The Taste for Beauty* (Cambridge: Cambridge University Press, 1989 trans. Carol Volk).

27 Jean-Marc Elsholz, '2001: *L'Odyssée de l'espace*, Le grand oeuvre', *Positif*, no. 439, September 1997.

28 Claude-Alexis Gras, in *Tausend Augen*, no. 10, August 1997.

29 [In addition to its cognate meanings, *alignement* in French commonly refers to alignments or ordered rows of prehistoric stones as monuments, for example the menhirs at Carnac. – Translator.]

30 Kubrick, in Agel, p. 80.

31 A few examples among many follow. The monolith's arrival among the apes: it is already there when we see it. Similarly, it is already there at the moon site when Floyd's group sees it. The launching of spaceships: the film does not show the Discovery's departure from earth.

32 This trope of turning towards (Leonardo di Caprio towards Kate Winslet under the clock), or seeing someone turn towards you, holds a considerable place in Dante's *Divine Comedy*, where the trope is very often associated with mystical and amorous ecstasy.

33 According to Françoise Dolto, the phallus is the symbol of the object the possession of which would be most satisfying. Recall that in the Lacanian psychoanalytical dialectic, a man does not 'possess' the phallus any more than does a woman.

34 This theme gives all its force, especially, to the future world of *Soylent Green* (1973), a post-*2001* film that suffers from a mediocre screenplay predicated entirely on the revelation at the end about what becomes of the corpses (they serve to feed an overpopulated humanity), but which gives this question an answer that is both monstrous and logical.

35 Lacan sees the psychoanalyst as the 'sujet-supposé-savoir', the person

supposed to have the knowledge, in the eyes of the patient who is the one who really does the work. The analyst does not have the knowledge of the patient and his/her unconscious, but the patient attributes this knowledge to the analyst.

36 Hal is identified by a red eye and a voice, the monolith by a mute and opaque shape. Critics have seen in the monolith 'a pure effect of cinematic *écriture*, [representing] the fade to black' (see Ghezzi, *Stanley Kubrick*, p. 90), referring to the death of Dave, during which the camera moves towards the object whose darkness takes over the screen.

37 Lacan, *Ecrits* (London: Routledge, 1980), pp. 187, 318–19.

38 According to Françoise Dolto, we carry in ourselves two parents: the 'continuous parent', which is the maternal role associated with continuity and security, and the 'discontinuous parent', the one who comes and goes, is not always present, who embodies and permits the process of symbolisation, who holds the role of the symbolic Father (whether a man or woman fills the role).

39 Dolto's neologism *mammaïser* means 'associate (through speech) with the reassuring figure of Mama'. If the little child fears a noise, for example the noise of a coffee grinder, and if the mother calms the child's fear with an explanation, s/he associates it with the security represented by the maternal universe. See Dolto, *Lorsque l'enfant paraît* (Paris: Éditions du Seuil, vol. 3, 1979, p. 53).

40 The confrontation with Hal shows a clear resemblance to the episode of the Cyclops Polyphemus in the *Odyssey*. But there are clear differences, too. In Homer, Polyphemus is blinded, not killed; he only kills some of Odysseus's companions; he is on his turf and holds Odysseus prisoner; Odysseus must use trickery not to enter but to leave. Finally, I have already pointed out the archery reference in the name Bowman; and in Homer Odysseus is famous for the bow he alone can shoot, and with which he kills the rivals for his wife Penelope. But the parallels remain spotty and vague.

41 '*Playboy* Interview: Stanley Kubrick' (1968), reprinted in Schwam, p. 298.

42 Ibid., loc. cit.

Chapter Six
Science-fiction Cinema after *2001*

2001's Soviet Brother: *Solaris*

In the wake of the splash created by the release of *2001*, but also because of outer space in the news, American science fiction took on a more technological and documentary aspect for a while. *Marooned* 1970, by John Sturges, with Gregory Peck, depicted the rescue of a space mission, while *The Andromeda Strain* (1971), directed by Robert Wise based on a novel by Michael Crichton, created an abstract kind of technological suspense. Douglas Trumbull, one of the key visual-effects men for *2001*, directed a slow and elegiac sci-fi odyssey in 1972, *Silent Running*, starring Bruce Dern. John Carpenter began his directing career with a good-natured parody of Kubrick's film called *Dark Star* (1974), one of whose protagonists is a computer that is very finicky. But it would take the global success of George Lucas's *Star Wars* in 1977 to bring about a new wave of science fiction, which has hardly ebbed since.[1]

One film project in particular, undertaken immediately after the release of Kubrick's, interests me for several reasons, and this is Tarkovsky's *Solaris*. It is undeniable that *Solaris* was born not only out of the genius of its director (who consistently claimed his dissatisfaction with it),[2] but also out of the desire by the chiefs of Soviet cinema to produce a film that could compete with *2001* financially and in terms of international artistic prestige. In some ways, *Solaris* is emblematic of the competitiveness that was in the air. Presented at Cannes in 1972, the film received a Special Prize, but the press as well as public reception was restrained. The tenacity of a Parisian art house, Le Seine, which screened it once a week regularly for several years, eventually permitted many people, including me, to discover this extraordinary work.

Tarkovsky's journal, in the French edition published by *Cahiers du cinéma* (31 January 1971), makes only one allusion to Clarke's novel, without even commenting on it. But it seems impossible to me that the Russian film-maker could not have known about Kubrick's film, since it was shown in Moscow.

Adapted from a beautiful novel by the Polish writer Stanslaw Lem and completed in 1972, Tarkovsky's film lends itself to a fascinating comparison with *2001*. On the surface the meanings of the two films are contradictory. Tarkovsky rather strikingly takes a stand against the idea of space travel and of any possibility of tearing oneself away mentally from Mother Earth.

Furthermore, *Solaris* has no mutation of the species, and no jubilation. Tarkovsky used Bach's organ chorale 'Ich ruf zu dir' ('I called to you') for the film's music. In contrast to the triumphant music of Richard Strauss, this choice symbolises the difference of approach, even for those who do not know the title and text of this plaintive chorale. It is a piece that almost trembles, and is infinitely melancholy – a music of lamentation, of regret, far removed from the Promethean mood set in *2001*.

While the heroes of *2001* break all ties with their earthly histories, those of *Solaris* encounter it in flesh and bone, literally, no matter how far they travel in the cosmos. Tarkovsky's hero finds himself again only by accepting his past in the person of a deceased ex-mistress, Hari, who perpetually comes to life again at his side, under the influence of an ocean-planet probing his memory.

The characters in *2001* correspond to the image many Europeans have of Americans: pioneers with no culture or memory, thoroughly immersed in the action immediately at hand. Quite to the contrary, Tarkovsky's space travellers take along handfuls of soil from their country, quote poems and surround themselves with music and books. The 'salon' of their orbital station, a museum to human culture dominated by a reproduction of Breughel's *Hunters in the Snow*, is the antithesis of the cold Hilton that Kubrick made as impersonal as possible. The two films, which I rank equally highly, do, however, affirm the same agnosticism, and the same impossibility of communicating with a hypothetical other species – a theme that Lem developed magnificently in several of his novels such as *Eden*. At the end of *Solaris*, the small chunk of human landscape floating on the ocean-planet reminds one significantly of the period bedroom in Kubrick, surrounded by noises of an other world, and which we imagine to be lost in the cosmos.

At the same time Tarkovsky seeks to create expressly earthly images, filming grasses that undulate beneath the water of a stream, or waves of traffic on Japanese highways: the same hidden mystery as Kubrick with his sublime optical effects in the Cosmic Trip sequence.

At the end of the line in both *2001* and *Solaris*, man fatally falls upon a fabricated or authentic 'earthly' world which is his point of departure, or resembles it. The heroes of these two films live in illusions, constructed and lost in the heart of the abyss, in order to avoid confronting its intolerable emptiness.

Audiovisual Liturgies

2001 spawned an extensive legacy in the American and world cinema. I do not consider the post-*2001* legacy to be the space operas like *Star Wars* (which openly reinvigorated the tradition of the epic fantasy, a genre Kubrick esteemed highly), even though imagery in space operas benefited from the vistas opened by Kubrick and his collaborators. Nor was it the multi-episode saga of *Planet of the Apes* (whose first instalment, directed remarkably well by Franklin J. Schaffner, came out just before *2001*).

The legacy is most persuasively carried on through 'experience films', the liturgies of time-sound-light like *THX 1138* (1971), a futuristic sci-fi film also by Lucas – which, interestingly, through its logorrhoea (as well as by the disorienting editing by Walter Murch, who co-wrote, edited and dubbed the movie), achieved an effect that resembles what *2001* achieved through its muteness. Among these 'liturgical' films we may count *Zardoz* (John Boorman, 1971), with its trip sequence, *Soylent Green* (Richard Fleischer, 1973), *Close Encounters of the Third Kind* (Steven Spielberg, 1977), *Eraserhead* (David Lynch, 1977) – a film Kubrick admired, and which we might call a 'bedroom *2001*',[3] due to the majestic way the camera films a bed or penetrates into a radiator – *Altered States* (Ken Russell, 1979), *Apocalypse Now* (Francis Coppola, 1979, especially the opening), *Blade Runner* (Ridley Scott, 1982), *Brainstorm* (1983) by *2001* collaborator Douglas Trumbull, *The Big Blue* (Luc Besson, 1988), *The Abyss* (James Cameron, 1989), *Contact* (Robert Zemeckis, 1996), and many others.

What they have in common is that whether or not they belong to the sci-fi genre, they seem to dream of attaining the status of absolute cinema: the experience of watching them is, even if only for the time of one sequence, a temporal liturgy.

Despite their diversity, each film is like *2001* in including one or more silent non-narrative sequences that border on abstraction, and constructed around a character entering another world. This might be a subterranean universe in Lucas, death to the strains of Beethoven's Pastoral Symphony, or to Grieg's *Peer Gynt* in Fleischer's film, going up the river in Coppola, penetrating to the bottom of abysses in Besson and Cameron, the experience of hallucinogenic substances with Ken Russell. Spielberg's 1982 *E.T.* and John Carpenter's *Starman* from 1984 both culminate in a veritable 'Ite missa est' played on great audiovisual pipe organs.

I have mentioned only fiction films so far. Curiously, and significantly, the Americans' historic moon landing has not yet inspired a single film based on that subject, as far as I know. But we might cite a couple of works that adapt real events and which still take Kubrick's work as a point of reference. *The Right Stuff* (Philip Kaufman, 1982) tells the story of the first pioneer of supersonic flight; *Apollo 13* (Ron Howard, 1996) re-creates a mission more recent than the moon landing, and manages to rehabilitate, humanise and glorify the space pilots. The intention in both was to show that pilots have to face real risks, and are not at all the cold professionals or laboratory monkeys that *2001* might suggest.

As we see, this amounts to a considerable number of works, and we have still only mentioned but a few. Now, just as it has not been our intention to ridicule pre-*2001* movies, we should do our utmost not to insult the necessarily uneven films that Kubrick's masterpiece 'inspired'. 'Not everybody can be Kubrick': such a notion might justify the failures of emulators, but also regrettably amounts to stigmatising the ambition.

Let us pause on several films that show the substantial influence of *2001*, often in the very way they struggle against it.

The stroke of genius of *Blade Runner* (1982), based on Philip K. Dick's novel *Do Androids Dream of Electric Sheep?*, is to propose a post-*2001* in reverse. The story is set in the year 2019 in an overpopulated city on earth, from which there is no escape (as in Curtiz's *Casablanca*, to which Ridley

Scott's film makes several allusions[4]). But this space is discovered by an eye in extreme close-up; and like Dave Bowman's, it too sees stars and reflects their splendour. But in *Blade Runner*, this eye that sees marvels is not at the end but at the very beginning, with the superb idea consisting of transposing the Cosmic Trip of *2001* into images that magnificently represent the spectacle of earth, summed up in what ought normally to be considered the very height of ugliness: a cityscape saturated with smog, surrounded by factories belching flames, but also all aglow with lights.

In many respects the android Roy Batty, played by Rutger Hauer, is, in a sinister form, a Dave Bowman having returned from the stars and from 'beyond the infinite'. His desire to tell and share his story ('If only you could see what I've seen, with your eyes', 'I've seen things you people wouldn't believe') obliges him to come down off his Nietzschean pedestal and ultimately to end as a man, at the very moment his lifetime comes to a halt.

In the pacifist tradition of Robert Wise's film *The Day the Earth Stood Still* (mentioned above and featuring benevolent aliens visiting our planet), *Close Encounters of the Third Kind* (1977, with Douglas Trumbull's help on special effects) is also a *2001* on earth. Its final sequence limits plot to the minimum in order to let us participate alongside the characters in a mass of sounds and lights. The major difference between *Close Encounters* and *2001* is that it is punctuated with many 'Oh my God's' of amazement, which get to be a bit much, though it is true that Spielberg's film is deliberately sentimental, helped along by the talent and the childlike look of Richard Dreyfuss.

The hero of *Le Grand bleu* (*The Big Blue*), played by Jean-Marc Barr, devoted to free-diving in the ocean, has the same smooth and impenetrable personality as Keir Dullea's Dave Bowman. Independently of my lack of enthusiasm for this film, which I find less inspired than other Besson films, I think that, in its way, *Le Grand bleu* was for one generation what *2001* was for mine. That is to say that it was a film where the emptiness of the screen, often occupied by large, simple shapes, allows us to project something on the order of the absolute into it, and at least Besson can be credited as a director who pursues his ideas to the fullest.

More generally, the stimulating influence of *2001* can be measured through the new positions and new sorts of challenges it created – such as the challenge of taking an opposing stance to *2001* in some way. *Star Wars* chose to show interstellar vehicles that are ultra-rapid, contrary to the majestic slowness of the Discovery and the Orion, and banged-up too, with dents and scratches foreign to the brand-new look of Kubrick's spacecraft. But it is *Alien* (Ridley Scott, 1979) (also shot in a British studio) that would perfect this look with its vessel Nostromo that looked like a wreck. In fact, Russian film-makers, including Tarkovsky, had preceded *Alien* in this trend of decrepit technology.

Finally, like many other successful works, *2001* eventually spawned a screen sequel, *2010*, and Arthur C. Clarke gave it two others in book form.

2010, the 'Sequel'

It would be easy to condemn the film Peter Hyams made in 1984, *2010*, adapted from Clarke's novel of the same name. Produced, written, conceived and directed much more traditionally, it came out in a decade abundant with science-fiction films, and had the difficult task of striking a compromise between the design of *2001* with its particular style and fetish-objects, and new possibilities that were becoming available to film-making. At the same time, considered on its own merits and not in the shadow of *2001*, it is not entirely lacking in good moments – the conversation at the beginning between the American and the Russian in a forest of radio-telescopes, and the scene of boarding the Discovery, filmed like a visit to a ghost ship. Its main fault resides in a plot that does not hang together. Most of all, the film fails to bring its predecessor to life, as some sequels have managed to do, whether we judge them equal to the originals or not (I am thinking here of the interesting *Psycho* series made after Hitchcock's death).

One of the best scenes is the sortie into outer space, where the film dares to take the reference to *2001* against the grain once again. Where Keir Dullea and Gary Lockwood accomplished their spacesuited mission with measured breathing and interchangeable gestures, John Lithgow plays a novice cosmonaut seized with panic when facing the interstellar void. The film at that point shows us someone who suffers and is afraid of dying, and we can really feel the concrete, physical experience he undergoes.

We should mention that Keir Dullea appears in *2010* in various guises as Bowman. As a guardian angel, for example, he comes to earth – a clean, ecological, high-tech earth – to invisibly visit his dying mother, before working 'hand in hand' with a Hal whose voice is, again, that of Douglas Rain. Roy Scheider takes over from William Sylvester in the much better developed role of Heywood Floyd; but the character, despite Scheider's acting talent, still does not have much to offer.

Another problem is that *2010*, the novel and the film, literally does not know what to do with the 'character' of Hal. We are made to await his resurrection as the defining moment of the drama; then once Hal 9000 is awakened through the work of his 'father', Doctor Shandra, the computer once again becomes an inconspicuous partner. Elsewhere, the monoliths lose their symbolic and mythic value, as they multiply like flies and appear like assembly-line tools made by the millions. Seeing several monoliths at once has the effect – no doubt planned this way – of making them banal, ordinary, since the question of their emergence and their disappearance no longer has the same sacred quality.

In *2010*, it is a characteristic turnaround that man does not 'conquer' the cosmos. On the contrary, a non-human species, still invisible but fantastically more powerful than us, comes to banish man from a portion of our own solar system, by putting the message 'Keep Out' on one of ex-Jupiter's moons. Man is not only cut off from the stars, but also banished from a sector of space in his own backyard.

2061: Odyssey Three, a novel by Clarke published in 1987 and not yet adapted for the screen (there is also a brand-new *3001: The Final Odyssey*), brings back Heywood Floyd yet again. Mathematically Floyd is more than 100 years old but biologically he is only 65, because of numerous hibernations he has been through. The story is about the rescue of a human crew stranded on the colonised planet Europa (a moon of Jupiter). Except for one isolated chapter, the story abandons any metaphysical ambitions and presents itself as a pure scientific entertainment, and as an exercise in futurology. We can say much the same about the recent book *3001*; there, contact with the aliens has still not occurred, but the author, from the perspective of the idyllic and peaceful fourth millennium he describes, settles old scores a bit too easily with religion and with the stupidity and bad faith of our waning 20th century.

But let us take care not to close off the future. Maybe this *2061* and this *3001* will make great films one day in the hands of some director to come, perhaps better even than Kubrick's, and why not? Isn't one of the messages left by *2001* that we must continue to open up avenues?

Notes

1   In the strict sense, *Star Wars* is not a futuristic science-fiction film, since the action is set 'a long time ago, in a far far galaxy'. But it places many elements of science fiction in a context of heroic fantasy.

2   Particularly in the course of an interview I had with him in 1983 for *Libération-Cahiers*, when Tarkovsky told us he would have liked to be able to remove all elements of technological science fiction.

3   See my book on David Lynch (*David Lynch* [London: BFI, 1995]), in which I discuss the influence of Kubrick on this director.

4   The searchlights that sweep through space, the exotic atmosphere in some streets, one or two interior scenes between Harrison Ford and Sean Young, the chéchia/fez and the 'levantine' accent of one minor character.

Chapter Seven
2001 and Eyes Wide Shut: Last Odyssey to Manhattan[1]

'I have to be completely frank.'

(Eyes Wide Shut)

I

First, a waltz. But unlike the triumphal major-key waltz by Johann Strauss that provided the signature of the space sequence and the closing credits of *2001*, we hear a beautiful, resigned waltz in a minor key, by Shostakovitch. It is a waltz made to human measure, which you might hum like a melancholy memory – it even has a voice, the voice of a saxophone accompanied by an orchestra – and which resolves calmly and ineluctably on the tonic. Then, finally, a solemn and funereal reprise, with the same melody and harmony, as if in homage to the permanence of ephemeral human existence.

This is the waltz of the everyday, expressing the pace of life itself. It recurs twice in the beginning and also over the end credits, like a discreet requiem.

There is a couple dancing in this last film by Kubrick, and it is no longer the pairing of a male space object and a female space object, or a monolith and stars. This dance, during an elegant ball at the home of the millionaire Ziegler against a backdrop of glittering lightbulbs, brings together the suave womaniser Szavost and a woman who is surely very beautiful, but also very real – at her bathroom washbasin (a place Kubrick frequently returns to) she is a far cry from the iconic image of female beauty.

While reminiscent of *2001*, *Eyes Wide Shut* thus informs us that we are very much on earth this time, in the concrete life of men and women, here and now. And that the waltz does not ennoble, does not elevate us in the

Nietzschean manner; and that this time, the waltz is an anthem of our fate as non-flying bipeds.

If one tries to make a distinction among Kubrick's films, between those in marching rhythm – a generally funereal march as in *Paths of Glory, Dr Strangelove, Barry Lyndon, A Clockwork Orange* and *Full Metal Jacket* – and the films in waltz rhythm (which are less numerous), then one concludes that *Eyes Wide Shut* and *2001* belong to the second group. Both are symbolised by a ternary rhythm.

This can be seen as Kubrick's final homage to the film-maker he admired most of all, Max Ophuls, and especially to the waltz of *The Earrings of Madame de* ...

Even though they differ so much in form (*Eyes Wide Shut* does not have the strong formal demarcations; the action takes place within a limited time frame; there are no intertitles; there are few foregrounding effects of structure; and the editing is as fluid as possible), I see *Eyes Wide Shut* and *2001* as twin films, two complementary works with the same subject: the mystery of existence.

One of the two is on the side of eternity, or at least a vast time span, and the other, on the side not of the ephemeral exactly but the present, the *hic et nunc*.

'*Forever*, let's not use that word, it frightens me,' says Alice Harford (Nicole Kidman) to her husband Bill (Tom Cruise) at the end of the film.[2] Eternity, that same eternity glimpsed at the end of *2001*, is always there, but suspended, in this period of waiting and transition in which the action of *Eyes Wide Shut* is set.

Mysteriously, *Eyes Wide Shut* is also the film whose temporal setting meets up with that of Kubrick's most futuristic work. *Eyes Wide Shut* was completed just before the narrative time frame of *2001*'s ending. It covers a short time span that hovers around the present, unlike *2001*'s vast range from once-upon-a-time, to a generation-into-the-future, to, well, eternity. But *Eyes Wide Shut* could take place in 2001 (cell phones, the design of cars, the AIDS menace) or in 1999, it is not important.

The Shining took place in a vague, depopulated present (the film contains hardly any images of contemporary life) with a sort of 20s air; *Full Metal Jacket* was an evocation of the 70s; *Dr Strangelove* locked us in with its military and political characters (where was daily life of the time?); and let us not talk about the director's historical films, which transport us to the First World War, Roman history or Thackeray's 18th century.

Even more than *The Killing*, *Killer's Kiss* or *Lolita*, *Eyes Wide Shut* is Kubrick's most 'terrestrial' film, the most firmly situated in the here and now of the period during which it was made. There is no imminent apocalypse on the horizon. Its cars move normally through the streets of Greenwich Village; some people are starting out in life and others are leaving it; daily newspapers appear, the bars are full of people, doctors are consulted; everyone does business or plays out their social role in front of or behind a window, as in everyday life.

The man who has just bought a newspaper, Bill Harford, could read this headline on the front page if he were not in such a hurry: 'Lucky to be alive'. But he never does. We spectators have paid a little more attention. The metaphysical question opened up by *2001* (what does it mean *to be*, and in particular, *to be human*) seems to boil down here to the concrete question of *being alive*. And on that topic, everyone knows what has happened: as Ziegler tells Bill, 'Someone died. It happens all the time. But life goes on. It always does. Until it doesn't.' These sentences are short, they could hardly be more lapidary and irrefutable.

'She got her brains fucked out, period,' also says the ambiguous Ziegler about the woman whose body Bill has seen. Here again, death is a *commutation*, an effect of discourse, from the state of living to the state of non-living. Early in the film, 'eyes wide open' are a pair of eyes that Bill Harford succeeds in re-opening through words; they belong to the beautiful girl with Ziegler who overdosed on drugs ('Can you open your eyes for me?' Bill says, delighted to play the hypnotist awakening his subject). And there are 'eyes wide shut' like the open eyes of the nude girl in the morgue, like the open eyes of any dead person before you shut them. Between the eyes wide open and eyes wide shut there is just this invisible passage that would be impossible to pinpoint in time. So death in Kubrick is a state that is predicated, stated, an effect of discourse, the 'before' and 'after' of a memory-less flick of the switch.

A masked master at the ritual orgy tells Bill, who claims to have forgotten the password, 'That's unfortunate. Because here, it doesn't matter whether you've forgotten it or if you never knew it,' all in one terrible sentence directly borrowed from Schnitzler's novella.

Another astonishingly prescient scene in *Eyes Wide Shut* shows a dead man on his bed looking as though he is still sleeping, like the astronauts in deep freeze and like Dave Bowman in *2001* – and like the official description of Kubrick's own death not long afterwards.[3]

But this time, a foetus does not glow above the bed of Lou Nathanson. Where did *2001*'s luminous child go, whose wide open and protruding foetal eyes do not yet see anything concrete? And could the 'eyes wide shut' of the title be, without a face behind them, the eyes of that mask occupying Bill Harford's place on the pillow of the conjugal bed – like the eyes of the future male child Alice would bear him?

It is through the eyes and ears of the yet unborn boy of Alice and Bill Harford that the last film by Kubrick is felt and told. This is my theory.

The scenes of the streets of the Village and Soho, partially reconstituted on indoor sets in London, strike us by their absolute truthfulness: they are scenes of life on earth. My point is that in these street scenes, the camera takes the position of a child to be born, waiting to be embodied, who is floating in the air and roving through life on earth. For me, the film is an imaginary sequel to *2001*, in which instead of facing off with the whole planet, the male seed, waiting to inhabit and grow in a woman's womb, waits and watches life, and witnesses multiple possibilities of unions and births, and finds itself catapulted into a cosmic space full of matrices. This is the space discussed by the Tibetan *Book of the Dead* where visions of males and females in sexual union appear to the spirit waiting to be reborn, visions as in Kubrick's scene of the mysterious orgy.

'When you see couples making love, you will have strong feelings of jealousy. If you are going to be reborn as a male, you will feel desire for the woman and hatred for the man.'[4]

The sinister and ritualised orgy in *Eyes Wide Shut* is the cosmic locus of general copulation, which every human on earth thinks about when s/he wonders about the chance factors of her/his own existence: How did my progenitors meet? Could I not have been born of other parents? Might I never have been born? A number of other film-makers have given us such scenes of balls, orgies, places of chance meetings, as symbolic representations of existence as a chain of aleatory collisions between men and women that voluntarily or otherwise lead to the creation of new lives. Think of Tati (*Jour de Fête, Monsieur Hulot's Holiday, Playtime*), Bertrand Blier (*Notre histoire Tenue de soirée*), the dances in Ophuls's *Earrings of Madame de . . . .*

Such a theory, whereby *Eyes Wide Shut* becomes the reverie of a male subject waiting to be embodied, merits, if not being proven (how could it be?), at least being fleshed out with some supporting ideas.

2

Let us first remark that *2001* and *Eyes Wide Shut* (whose story is set just before Christmas) are from beginning to end two films dominated by the idea of prologues, 'beforeness', Advent.[5] Something is about to happen, in the form of a cycle, that we hope opens out into a spiral; always a new era, a new year, a new millennium (Kubrick finished his film in 1999). At the end of *2001*, a foetus, a miraculous male child, was confronting earth and our gaze. At the end of *Eyes Wide Shut*, more trivially and modestly, Santa Claus is coming to bring presents to boys and girls, in honour of a divine child born before the year turns over and begins anew.

From the opening of the film, there are countless Christmas trees in everyone's houses – the prostitute's apartment, the house where a man lies dead on his bed, the Harfords' living room, the hospital lounge, put us into the space of this magical pre-Christmas; and at the ball, thousands of electric bulbs illuminate the beauty of Nicole Kidman as if in a dream.

A scene cut from *2001* showed Heywood Floyd videophoning from the space station to Macy's to order a bushbaby toy as a present for his young daughter. This promise of a present for a little girl – a promise never kept in the context of the film – is found again at the end of *Eyes Wide Shut*. The movie ends in a toy store, with two kinds of waiting in progress: for a toy that will be bought by little Helena's parents (baby stroller, stuffed bear?), and for sex between the man and wife.

Let us imagine that little Helena receives as a 'present' (this word is often used by parents, rather perversely, to explain to their child that a baby is on the way) something even better than the giant teddy bear she covets: a baby brother. A baby she could put in the stroller, for example, that she has seen in the store.

This is not such a far-fetched idea. Why, after all, does Alice Harford make her declaration to her husband ('We have to fuck') in a store decked out for Christmas?

If we see it this way, then Kubrick spent no less than thirty years, between 1968 and 1999, trying to come through on a promise of a gift to a child. It is as if he regretted having left the promise of the bushbaby toy – a baby after all – up in the air, and that this had haunted him the whole time.

So the later film appears to rest on one promise and on one little girl's expectation. This will astonish only those who do not take films – and promises made to children – literally enough. In fact, it is strange how people do not take films, and humans, literally.

Consider how the film begins and how it ends.

The first image in *Eyes Wide Shut*, inserted via sharp, clean cuts between two titles, is one that could appear banal in some movies but which in a movie like this cannot be banal: Alice Harford, Nicole Kidman, her back to the camera, slips off her dress and is briefly seen nude.

She is standing straight, her dress is black, her back and her thighs are magnificent. And in a way, she is the monolith, the phallus-body that unveils itself, and which once unveiled is none the less impenetrable or infrangible.

This body of Nicole Kidman becomes the object that crystallises the film; it disappears from the central section, but it haunts the fantasies of her husband.

While other films by Kubrick begin or end with an eye (*A Clockwork Orange*) or a penetrating through space (*The Shining*), his last work begins with the object *par excellence*, the Thing, the feminine body.[6]

As for the final image: it shows us Nicole Kidman once again, addressing her husband, but it is only her face, adorned with glasses, articulating one word, 'fuck'. One of these succinct, percussive monosyllables that English is good at; and which is rapidly followed by a cut to the closing credits. Again, there is no pausing, no fade-out: there is just before and after.

The humour in this is that it comes at the end of such a long and involved film that maddeningly takes its time, a film narrated and developed with great patience, stage by stage, which spares us none of its periods of dead time, none of the waiting. At the very end comes this moment where the

heroine suddenly realises something she and her husband must do as soon
as possible. ASAP. And the final cut falls on the film like a guillotine blade.

Such is life: we take all the time in the world, which gives way to a sense
of urgency and immediacy as we near the end.

The time to walk from one place to another; the time spent waiting for
something; the time between one sentence and the next that turns out
merely to repeat the first (a considerable number of lines in *Eyes Wide Shut*
do this); the time between words that are spoken by two people, into which
a sexual current insinuates itself and into which is sketched the story they
could live – this time, of which Kubrick is the cinematic master, and which
he organises with immense care and love, ends up being cancelled, forgotten, redeemed in the reunion of the couple and in the editing that both
cuts and settles on the word 'fuck' in an instant.

I find it reasonable to see the film as being situated between the first
image of a person stripping, and the last *word* that proposes a sexual act
(and which the movie's abrupt ending leaves the spectator to imagine or,
if s/he desires, to act on ...).

But in Kubrick, the image of the woman is not just for men's eyes. She
is also an image for herself, as should be evident in the shot of the nude
couple that was used for the film's ad campaign: having removed her
glasses, Alice glances toward the mirror in which we see her reflection.

In *2001*, the mirror does not enter the picture until the end, when the
man discovers himself as an other, as if he is his own rival. Here Alice looks
at herself in the mirror, but could it be a third person she looks at, rather
than herself? Or might she be daydreaming?

Watching *2001*, we asked, what is the monolith thinking about, how can
we get inside it? Here, the question is: what is a woman thinking about
while embracing her husband? After all, even and especially when she is
disrobing, a woman does not give herself over, everyone knows this. Or at
least, that is what all movies tell us. The image of Alice's sidelong glance
in the mirror opens all the doors of ambiguity.

The man's jealousy takes root in his suspicion that during lovemaking,
the woman is thinking of someone else, of the 'handsome navy officer' of
his fantasy – and the man is thus fated always to be for the woman the
shadow of another man, or of God.

'The shadow of God,' writes Françoise Dolto, 'isn't every man the shadow of God for a woman who loves her man?'[7]

Or if the sexual union Alice asks Bill for, and which is unresolved at the end, was fertile and impregnated her with a male child, the baby would not fail to be the magical and absolute rival.

To have a baby boy is a wrenching dilemma for certain fathers. On the one hand, it fulfils them by providing them an heir with their name, and in confirming their masculine pride. On the other, this boy and his penis, who has come out of the belly of their wife, this boy fated to detest them, as the Tibetan *Book of the Dead* said well before Freud, is their absolute rival.

The mask in Alice's bed when Bill returns home at the end is perhaps the foreshadowing of this, of the magical child who will replace him and fulfil the woman.

I am also thinking of the extraordinary shot in *Eyes Wide Shut* showing Carl, the fiancé of Lou Nathanson's daughter (played by Thomas Gibson), making his way to the room where the dead man lies on a bed. He has exactly the same gestures, the same walk and the same way of knocking on the door, and he is followed by the same camera movement as Bill was several minutes earlier in the same place. It is as if, in occupying the same space and making the same gestures, this apparently insignificant young man were there solely in order to knock Bill Harford like a billiard ball up into the next older age bracket. As if Bill were doomed to be wiped out soon himself, and had no 'next position' other than death.

The brilliant shot transitions at the end of *2001*, in which the man seems to foreshadow his own older self, could be seen as the reverse of this process whereby the son displaces the father whose gestures he reproduces, knocking him into old age.

Fortunately, recalls Alice at the end of the film, maybe it was all just a dream, and both of them must be grateful for surviving.

Even if it means that Bill has to give Alice the magical child who will jostle him into his death.

3

Finally, *2001*'s way of providing the ultimate explanation of the mystery was to leave us with two brief formal speeches by Floyd – one live, for the researchers of Clavius, the other prerecorded. *Eyes Wide Shut* no longer beats about the bush; it offers us one of the strangest sequences of explanation in the cinema, in the extraordinary sequence in the billiard room between Ziegler (Sydney Pollack) and Bill (Tom Cruise).

In this scene, which takes place around a pool table – symbolic surface of both aleatory and controlled collisions, guided by laws, and a both cosmic and sexual symbol where one has to figure out what ball will fall into what hole – a man who speaks bluntly plays the role of the father, stating and at the same time rendering trite the mysteries of life and death, scolding and reassuring, threatening but also apologising, explaining and revealing, clarifying the interdiction but also challenging its logic, all with the most total ambiguity possible.

2001 depends entirely on logical connections and on the absence of explanation; its sections are tied together by the very absence of words in the presence of enigmatic editing. *Eyes Wide Shut*, on the other hand, is centred on a long and disturbing scene of revelations, during which verbal explanations get us deeper into mystery and doubt than their absence did. This is the reverse and the complement of *2001*.

As it happens, the 'last word' Ziegler can say to explain the death of a woman and solve the mystery of her dying, is to pronounce a punctuation mark: period. Language is reduced to a void, to the pure sign.[8]

In a way, we never escape the verbal, nor do we escape the non-sense of the signifier. Kubrick was aware of this; towards the end of his career he showed a fondness for oxymoronic titles, which are 'switch-throwing' montages of words. Clockwork orange, full metal jacket, eyes wide shut: these three are made out of juxtapositions of a word for a mechanical, hard, closed, discontinuous element (clockwork, metal, shut) with an organic, open, flexible, continuous element.

There is something here that can never be totalised nor explained. But at least Kubrick left behind, to tell of the mystery of our life on earth and the eternal story of man and woman, a work both enigmatic and human, concrete and metaphysical, benevolent and fraternal, as his final creation, after which he could die, before the year 2000's resetting to zero, and one year later, the new millennium on the threshold of which he had placed his monolith, 2001.

2001, this title of a new beginning, where two blind eyes, widely open or shut, fix us in their gaze.

Notes

1   A large part of the preceding text was written before Stanley Kubrick's death and the release of *Eyes Wide Shut*.

  Rather than pepper the essay with footnotes, I have preferred to write an additional chapter that is also a homage to Kubrick. It also seems to me that the two films share a close relationship.

2   In the original novel by Schnitzler, *Eine Traumnovelle*, the word comes from the mouth of the male character, but the woman puts her finger on his lips before he utters it. Kubrick, a courageous Icarus, always ready to tempt fate, challenges superstition by having Alice say it out loud. He died immediately after finishing the film.

3   The detail 'died in his sleep' was added to the adaptation. In the Schnitzler, the death is caused by a heart attack, which might have taken place while the man was awake and conscious.

4   Stephen Hodge and Martin Boord (eds), *The Illustrated Tibetan Book of the Dead* (New York: Godsfield Press, 1999).

5   In French, *Avent*, Advent, the period of awaiting the birth of Jesus in the Christian calendar, is a homonym of *avant*, the word for 'before'.

6   [Chion is speaking in psychoanalytic terms here: the body of the mother, for the child. He is also referring to female body as the object of the male look. Throughout, he is characterising the *symbolic representation* of the body as it exists in the film. – Translator.]

7   Françoise Dolto, *L'Evangile au risque de la psychanalyse* (Paris: Éditions Jean-Pierre Delarge, 1977), vol. 1, p. 23. Godard quotes her formulation in *Hail Mary* (1984). At the beginning of the Gospel of St Luke, the archangel Gabriel announces to Mary that 'The Holy Spirit will come upon you, and the power of the Most High will overshadow you' (Luke 1:35).

8   Consider also the sudden and deliberately vulgar noise Ziegler makes with his mouth to indicate how a woman went from being alive to being dead.

Appendix I
2001: Breakdown by Scenes

Opening Titles: an Alignment of Celestial Bodies
Sound: music of *Thus Spake Zarathustra*.

A. Title: The Dawn of Man

A1. Before the Monolith (approx. 6´49´´)
Series of shots showing deserted landscape, as dawn breaks.

A small group of apes; they feed on sparse vegetation, alongside a peaceful herd of tapirs. They fear the attacks of a tiger. They live in clans, with a leader. They exchange challenges and war cries with another clan who compete for their watering hole. At night they live in fear of predators, represented by the growling of wild beasts in the darkness and by a leopard that stalks them.

Sound: natural sounds and growling; no music. Visual transitions: three fade-outs – after a leopard attack, after the scuffle with the rival clan and to mark the passage of time.

A2. The Apes and the Monolith (approx. 2´43´´)
One morning, the leader of the ape group (Dan Richter), the first of the clan to awaken, notices the presence of a black parallelepiped that has been erected, perhaps 10–12 feet tall. The group circles round it with high-pitched cries, and some apes draw closer, even daring to touch it.

Sound: ape cries; the Ligeti *Requiem* gradually fades up over their cries. Music is suddenly cut off simultaneously with the image of the monolith, to lead to A3.

A3. After the Monolith, the Idea (approx. 2′15″)

Soon, the monolith gone now, the ape leader, digging around in a pile of tapir bones, gets the idea of using a bone as an instrument to hit other bones, and smashes them. (His idea, suggests the editing, is inspired by the memory of the monolith.) He also gets the idea (suggested by a subjective shot of a live tapir falling down) to use it as a weapon to kill the animal.

Sound: quiet natural ambient noises; music of *Zarathustra* over the 'birth of the idea' and the discovery of the tool.

A4. After the Idea, Carnivorous Apes (approx. 1′04″)

The apemen eat raw meat.

Sound: wind and slight noise of carnivorous chewing; no music.

A5. The First Weapon (approx. 1′40″)

Around a watering hole, a violent clash between the two clans. The tribe whose story we are following uses the bone-weapon to gain the advantage over the other tribe and kill their leader. In a gesture of triumph and jubilation, the leader throws the bone up in the air; the bone begins to fall in slow motion . . .

Sound: horrendous ape cries, blows of the weapon striking the bodies of adversaries, then the cries fade and are lost in a light wind.

B. (No Title)

B1. Outer Space: the Flight of the Orion (approx. 5′20″)

. . . but in its place, we see a long, narrow spacecraft floating in space. Above the earth, in a sky in which various types of elongated space objects are moving, a spaceship streamlined like an arrow, piloted by a crew of two men, approaches a space station shaped like a wheel.

In the spaceship, the sole passenger (William Sylvester), strapped into his seat, sleeps in zero gravity. A stewardess (Penny Brahms) retrieves a pen that has escaped from the passenger's hand and is floating in the air.

The ship docks at the station and enters its landing bay . . .

Sound: symphonic rendition of the 'Blue Danube' Waltz; no speech or other sound of any kind.

B2. Inside the Space Station (approx. 7'53'')

The man is greeted in the space station by the chief of security. He goes through a voiceprint identification, a sort of customs. We learn he is the American Professor Floyd, that he has been there before, that he is on his way to the moon, to the American base of Clavius, and he has a one-hour layover. He picture-phones his little daughter back on earth (Vivian Kubrick) to wish her happy birthday. She asks for a present: first a telephone, and then, when her father tells her that they already have many, a bushbaby toy.[1] He has a conversation at the bar with some Russian scientists, three women including his friend Elena (Margaret Tyzack), and a man, Smyslov (Leonard Rossiter); the Russians and Americans have separate colonies on the moon. Through the conversation we learn that there are rumours of an epidemic in Clavius. Floyd denies this, but the Russians are sceptical.

Sound: dialogue and unobtrusive ambient noise; discreet announcements on a loudspeaker; no mechanical or electronic noises of telephone; no music. Visual transition: rapid fade-out at the end on the Russians who continue to talk after Floyd has left.

B3. Space: the Flight and Moon Landing of Aries[2] (approx. 7')

Floyd catches his flight in a round ship to a base on the moon; the ship is brought by a sort of elevator into an immense sub-lunar hangar. During his flight, we see a stewardess (Edwina Caroll), who in order to serve in-flight meal trays to the crew and passengers, walks in zero gravity by wearing bootees with Velcro soles that stick to the floor.

Sound: like B1, but another section of the Strauss waltz that concludes with a cadence. We see, without hearing, Floyd talking with the Aries' personnel.

B4. Floyd's Speech on Clavius (approx. 4'19'')

In a conference room on the base, Floyd is received by astronauts who work on Clavius, including Professor Ralph Halvorsen (Robert Beatty). They have been forced by circumstance to break all communications with earth and their families. He speaks to them, finally revealing that the rumour of an epidemic is a cover story to prevent the leak of a landmark discovery in the history of science, likely to have a profound impact on the world, and needing to be kept secret until the National Council of Astronautics decides on a course of action. Sent by the Council, Floyd has come to study the situation in person and write up a report that will be of help in deciding when and how to reveal the discovery. To a question from Professor Bill Michaels (Sean Sullivan), he declares that he has no idea what the Council will do.

Sound: dialogue, no music; no sound effects with dialogue.

B5. On the Moon: the Flight to the Monolith (approx. 5′03″)
During a low-altitude flight in a moon bus over the craters, we learn, through a conversation between Floyd, Michaels and Halvorsen, that the unearthed object was apparently 'deliberately buried', that it is four million years old, and emits a very strong magnetic field. The bus lands near an illuminated excavation site around the object.

Sound: music at the beginning, Ligeti's *Lux aeterna*, briefly mixed with dialogue at first; a muffled, continuous ambient sound is associated with the machinery of the bus; end of segment has a reprise of the *Lux aeterna*.

B6. On the Moon: Humans and the Monolith (approx. 3′35″)
Men in spacesuits, including Floyd, walk on the lunar surface and descend in a line toward the monolith. Floyd extends his hand to touch the enigmatic object. One of them is about to photograph the group in front of the object, but a high strident tone is heard deafeningly in their helmets, coinciding with the appearance of the sun.

Sound: no dialogue; reprise of Ligeti *Requiem*, cut off by very high continuous sound, itself cut off at the same time as the shot of the monolith, before the title card of the third section.

C. Title: Jupiter Mission: 18 Months Later
C1. Discovery: Mission I (silent exposition) (approx. 3′42″)
We discover another very large spaceship, very elongated in form with an antenna dish in the middle. It is equipped with a centrifuge to create gravity. In this centrifuge a man later identified as Frank Poole (Gary Lockwood) jogs in shorts and shadow-boxes as he goes, while three others

are hibernating in white coffin-like containers. The second waking human of the crew, later identified as Dave Bowman (Keir Dullea), joins Poole, who, after his physical exercise, is eating his meal, and Dave sits down next to him at the table.

Sound: music, Khachaturian's *Gayaneh*; no speaking; breathing of the man who is jogging and shadow-boxing.

C2. Discovery: Mission II (exposition in the form of televised programme) (approx. 4'45'')

From a televised programme retransmitted to them and watched by the astronauts during their meal, we learn that the spaceship Discovery was launched from earth three weeks ago, bound for Jupiter; that the active men are Dave Bowman and his first mate Frank Poole; and that the functions of the ship are managed by a computer of the series Hal 9000, who speaks with a suave and distinguished masculine voice (Douglas Rain), which talks with the humans, and which sees through cyclops-like red eyes installed throughout the ship. In the TV interview programme, Hal voices his satisfaction with working for the mission and being fully occupied. It is explained that the three other astronauts, Charles Hunter, Jack Kimball and Victor Kaminsky, were put into hibernation to save resources on board, and will be awakened once the vessel approaches its landing on Jupiter. The television interviewer asks if they attribute emotions to Hal.

Sound: dialogue – voices of BBC reporter, Frank, Dave and Hal on the programme; brief diegetic music signature of the BBC show; the characters present watch the programme in silence; muted sounds of air circulation in the ship.

C3. Discovery: Frank's Birthday; the Chess Game (approx. 3'10'')

While Dave sleeps, Frank, lying down for a tanning session attended to by Hal, receives the weekly recorded message from his parents on earth. They give him news[3] and wish him a happy birthday; later, Frank plays a game of chess with Hal, and loses.[4]

Sound: dialogue between Hal and Frank, and voices in the recorded birthday message mixed with the music that has been present since the beginning of the segment: Khachaturian's *Gayaneh*.

C4. Discovery: Hal Questions Dave and Predicts the Antenna Failure
(approx. 3′27″)

While Frank is sleeping, upon Hal's request Dave shows Hal pictures he
has been drawing of the hibernating astronauts. Then Hal questions
Dave about rumours preoccupying him concerning the 'mission', the
enigma of an object unearthed on the moon and the mystery of the three
astronauts, asleep before the take-off, even though they had been trained
for the flight. Dave does not answer. After excusing himself, Hal informs
Dave that an antenna unit on the Discovery will fail within seventy-two
hours.

Sound: dialogue Hal/Dave and muted ambient noise of the Discovery;
continuation and ending of *Gayaneh* over the beginning of the segment;
then no more music for the rest of section C.

C5. Space: Dave Does a Spacewalk to Replace the Antenna Unit
(approx. 7′55″)

After tests he conducts with Frank, and communicating with men at the
earth base who authorise them to replace the part, Dave puts on his spacesuit and readies a space pod to exit from the Discovery. Once out in the
pod, he goes out into the void, powered by a rocket backpack, in order to
remove the faulty antenna unit and replace it with a new one. Frank
watches the manoeuvre from the Discovery.

Sound: no dialogue or music, except at the beginning, when the mission
director speaks from earth, and when Dave orders Hal by voice to ready the
pod; then, 'objective-internal' sounds of breathing and the hissing of oxygen.

C6. Discovery: the Antenna Check; Hal Denies Making an Error
(approx. 3′58″)

In the Discovery, Dave and Frank examine the antenna and find no
defects; this finding is corroborated by a report from Mission Control on
earth. Hal has made a mistake. When asked, Hal maintains that this is
impossible and the problem must be human error. He suggests putting the
original antenna unit back in place and awaiting the breakdown so as to
be able to locate the cause;[5] Dave and Frank accept this proposal. After
an interrogation in which Hal reaffirms that he is incapable of error, Dave

and Frank look at each other; Dave asks Frank to accompany him to check out a problem in one of the pods.

Sound: dialogue; muffled ambient sounds of the Discovery, except in the pod when Frank and Dave have acoustically isolated themselves; no music.

C7. Discovery: Conspiring (approx. 4'09'')

Dave and Frank reach the area where the pods are stored. They hole up in a pod, and make certain to cut off all channels to Hal's 'ears' so they can talk. They agree that the computer might have a problem and they bring up the possibility of disconnecting Hal's intelligence circuits and keeping only the automatic circuits going, if it becomes clear that Hal is malfunctioning. They discuss the problems this will cause, not least of which would be Hal's reaction. Through a subjective shot, we see that Hal, although he cannot hear the astronauts, watches them talking through the pod porthole.

Sound: dialogue; no music; muffled rumbling of the Discovery on the shot of Hal's eye.

Intermission (music: Ligeti's *Atmosphères*)
C8. In Space: the Murder of Frank (approx. 2'33'')

Frank takes a pod out into space to reinstall the suspect antenna unit, while Dave follows the manoeuvres on a monitor inside the Discovery. But the pod, under Hal's remote command, turns against Frank and, with the pincers that are its 'arms', attacks him, and cuts the air-supply cable. Frank struggles, and flies off into the void, then floats away, presumably a dead body inside the spacesuit.

Sound: no dialogue or music; 'objective-internal' sounds of breathing and hissing, ceasing with the death of Frank and giving way to an absolute silence – the first in the film – on the exterior shots of space. Visual transition: three jump-cuts on the arrival of the malevolent pod attacking Frank.

C9. In Space: Retrieving Frank's Body (approx. 5'27'')

Having watched helplessly as the accident occurred without knowing what has caused it, Dave exits the Discovery control room in haste without taking his helmet. He takes out another pod in order to recover Frank's body, which he succeeds in rounding up with the articulated arms of the vehicle.

Sound: no music; brief dialogue in the Discovery between Hal and Dave at the beginning; then various diegetic sounds for the shots taken inside the pod; absolute silence on the shots filmed from the exterior.

C10. Discovery: the Murder of the Three Hibernating Astronauts (approx. 1′57″)

On board, Hal puts an end to the vital functions of the sleeping astronauts;[6] the line graphs monitoring their life functions go flat; electronic tones are heard and read-outs flash on screens: 'Computer malfunction', then 'Life functions endangered', then 'Life functions terminated'.

Sound: no speech or music, rhythmic beeps, then muffled continuous background noise of the Discovery over the final monitor message.

C11. Discovery and Space: Dave and Hal's Last Dialogue (approx. 2′36″)

From the pod, Dave asks Hal to open the Discovery pod-bay doors. Hal refuses, and argues for the greater good of the mission. He reveals to Dave that he knew about their intention to disconnect him for, in spite of their precautions, he read their lips. Then he ends their conversation and no longer answers Dave's orders.

Sound: dialogue Hal/Dave, whose beginning is heard 'on the air'; no music.

C12. Discovery and Space: Dave Abandons Frank's Body and Re-enters the Discovery Manually (approx. 5′57″)

In order to get back into the Discovery, Dave does a series of daring and risky technical manoeuvres that might allow him to re-enter through the airlock. But beforehand, to liberate the pod's arms, he must abandon the spacesuit containing the remains of Poole, the very reason he went out into space in the first place. He commands the manual opening of an airlock, and is violently sucked in, helmet-less, exposed briefly to the vacuum of space. He secures the door and flips the air on, and is safely back in the Discovery.

Sound: segment without dialogue or music; sounds of manoeuvre, with beeps and alarms in the pod, absolute silence on the exterior shots; silence, then rush of air in the Discovery airlock. Visual transitions: dissolve at the end between the eye of Hal and the silhouette of Dave walking towards the memory functions of the computer.

C13. Discovery: the Death of Hal, and Floyd's Prerecorded Message (approx. 7'08'')
Now with his space helmet on, Dave walks towards the chamber containing Hal's memory circuits, which is without gravity. He disconnects the computer in spite of Hal's pleas; Hal asks Dave to calm down, apologises, then pleads, then finally regresses to the point of singing a song that he was taught at his 'birth'. Once Hal is unplugged, a prerecorded message from Floyd begins on a monitor in the circuit chamber, informing Dave of the real goal of the mission, which only Hal knew: the monolith found on the moon that was sending signals towards Jupiter, and whose function has remained a mystery.

    Sound: Hal's monologue, heard with the same audio perspective and proximity no matter where Dave has been; breathing; hissing of air, and brief dialogue line of Dave in his helmet; Hal's song, plunging into increasingly low register. Visual transition: brief fade-out at the end.

D. Title: Jupiter and Beyond the Infinite
(This section is without dialogue throughout.)

D1. The Monolith Appears in Alignment with Jupiter and its Moons, Opening of the Discovery (approx. 4'41'')
Views of Jupiter and its moons. As if telecommanded from the exterior, the Discovery opens up, and the pod exits from it. The monolith, or a monolith, appears, floating horizontally, impossible to gauge its scale. The camera tilts up towards the starry sky.

    Sound: no dialogue; music: the 'Kyrie' from Ligeti's *Requiem*, leading into Ligeti's *Atmosphères*, mixed with rumbling.

D2. Dave's 'Cosmic Trip': Symmetrical Light Patterns (approx. 2'09'')
As if seen from the staring eyes of Dave, first we see symmetrical light pat-

terns that recede on the left and right borders of the frame, then to the top and bottom borders. Dave, inside, being more and more violently shaken by the travel, seems to be captured in a momentous, vertiginous trip into a different outer space.

Sound: Ligeti's *Atmosphères* and rumbling; the images that go by come out from the image's centre which was until then occupied by stars.

D3. Dave's 'Cosmic Trip': Masses of Stars and Chemical Forms; Stars in the Shape of a Diamond (approx. 3′47′′)

Then a nova that explodes, a galaxy, a sun, coloured and slowly moving forms whose scale is indeterminate, and which could be microscopic phenomena as easily as cosmic objects. Then coloured forms shaped like diamonds, then planar 'walls' that recede to the top and bottom borders of the field.

Sound: Ligeti's *Atmosphères*, rumbling.

D4. Dave's 'Cosmic Trip': Flying over Landscapes (approx. 2′53′′)

Then images suggesting vast, unearthly landscapes being flown over, in extraordinary colors, in which we recognise canyons, valleys, mountains, surfaces of lakes, frozen land or sea, volcanic phenomena.

Sound: Ligeti's *Atmosphères*, rumbling.

D5. Bedroom: Arrival of the Pod (approx. 2′40′′)

The pod is now ... in a huge luxury hotel suite in Regency-period style, hermetically sealed and lit from under the floor, surrounded by very reverberant noises. We think there is another man there ... but it is Dave himself, but much older, in his spacesuit and helmet. He explores the suite, enters a bathroom, sees himself in the mirror. We hear a sound of someone else's presence; Dave turns around ...

Sound: noise of formless, very reverberant sounds with sounds resembling voices (choirs? female voices?), and Dave's breathing. Towards the end of this segment, when the noise of human presence becomes more defined – they are the sounds of cutlery on a plate, of someone dining alone – the noise and the 'internal-objective' breathing gradually die down.

D6. Bedroom: Dave's Life in the Room; the Man Eating (3´28´´)

And he comes back towards the main room; a man is there in a robe. It is Dave himself, even older, who eats, turns round, then slowly rises and comes towards us, looks in the bathroom to see if anyone is in there, then, as if he has ascertained no one is there, sits down again at his luxuriously appointed dining table. He accidentally knocks a wine glass to the floor, where it breaks. He turns towards the bed when he hears breathing . . .

Sound: the noise and breathing gradually fade down; the sounds of dining become clearer and occupy the soundtrack alone; sounds of Dave in his robe, very reverberant as if in a well: the chair he pushes away that scrapes against the floor, the reverbed footsteps, the sounds of Dave and the clatter of breaking glass.

D7. Bedroom: the End of Dave and the Return of the Monolith (approx. 1´28´´)

. . . and sees a strange human form lying on the large bed; but it is Dave himself again, very old and bald, with laboured breathing; he slowly raises his arm towards something offscreen. It is the monolith, standing facing his bed. A shape resembling a glowing foetus becomes visible on the bed. The camera dollies in towards the monolith, as if it were moving through a black portal.

Sound: breathing; then the beginning of *Zarathustra*.

D8. Space: the Star Child (approx. 1´10´´)

The moon then planet earth; a light like that of another planet of equivalent scale enters from the left: it is the head of a gigantic foetus, which resembles Dave; it looks at the earth, then turns little by little towards us . . .

Sound: music of *Zarathustra*; image: fade to black on the foetus watching us.

End Titles (approx. 3´53´´)

Titles on black background; sound: orchestral music of 'Blue Danube' Waltz.

Note: the timings supplied are approximate, owing to variations in the state and nature of copies of the film, but also because of the more or less arbitrary choices we may make to see in one shot rather than in another, or even in the middle of another, the beginning or ending of a given scene.

Notes

1   In the French dub of *2001*, the animal that Floyd's daughter asks for is a little white rabbit. In the subtitled version, it's an *'ouistiti'* (marmoset). The translations are not arbitrary, of course: they seek to render the familiar and childlike aspect of the bushbaby which is a fuzzy, koala-like stuffed toy.

2   Aries is the name supplied in the photos and script for the shuttle to the moon.

3   This news is quite specific and resituates our heroes in everyday detail: popularity of Poole and Bowman on earth, pride of their parents; someone named Ray has had an attack of lumbago; what present to give to Elaine and Bill on behalf of Frank; the students of Mrs Poole (who is a schoolteacher) also send birthday wishes; the head of accounting in Houston has confirmed Poole's pay raise ...

4   This game has been analysed, based on the pieces showing on the screen, and it has been established that Poole could perfectly well win. The possibility of playing chess with a computer already existed in the 60s, but was quite a novelty. Advances in personal computers made human v computer chess games an everyday affair, beginning in the late 70s.

5   The irony of the screenplay is that this proposition, born of insane logic, is accepted by the human characters without flinching, and accepted by the audience too. Dave has just braved the dangers of outer space to install a new antenna that has no possible flaws.

6   Of course, we do not 'see' Hal doing this. The spectator deduces this from the shots presented. The same goes for the murder of Frank in scene C8.

Appendix 2
French Press Release

Here is the (unsigned) release, obviously approved if not written by Kubrick, that was included in the French press kit upon the release of *2001* in France. Note that the text anticipates a human moon landing in the 70s (which in fact occurred in 1969). Note also that it invites the spectator to identify in turn with Heywood Floyd and with the Jupiter Mission's astronauts, without supplying specific names of characters.

Neither the character of Hal nor the 'Dawn of Man' prologue is mentioned. The characters are representative of all humanity (the masculine pronouns are the French equivalent of the neuter or impersonal in English).

Less than an hour ago, you took off in a rocket from the Kennedy spaceport in New York on a trip that will take you to the farthest corners of the universe.

Your first stop is the slowly rotating wheel of Space Station 5, which is orbiting very far above the Equator. You land at the space colony three kilometres in diameter to await the shuttle to the moon.

While you wait in the spacious observation area, you have a breathtaking view of the earth. This dazzling spectacle passes before your eyes twice per minute, since the space station is revolving like a cosmic carousel. The centrifugal force generated by its rotation gives you the sensation of normal gravity: you can walk on the curved floor, you can pour something to drink knowing that the liquid will stay in the glass, you can tell up from down.

Exactly two days from now, you will be on the moon, this formerly inaccessible world, to confront a mystery that has surged up from the past, and which now is mystifying the most highly trained minds of the twenty-first century . . .

Your shuttle has crossed the abyss of more than 400,000 kilometres that was conquered for the first time by astronauts in the 1970s. In the crater Clavius, more than 240 kilometres wide, you are welcomed by scientists at the recently built space research station. This is a small underground colony, almost entirely self-sufficient so that it no longer needs supplies from Mother Earth. Children have already been born here who know no other country; the Clavius base is the first human colony in another world. Here, scientists are uncovering the moon's secrets and are learning methods of survival on even more hostile planets.

Several hours later, you sail far above the lunar plains, making your way towards a faraway scientific outpost in the huge crater of Tycho. And there, in this solitary encampment in the middle of the lunar desert, you find yourself facing a mystery that will shake the world: you find the first sign that Man is not alone.

You are now further away from home than any man has ever been.

For nine months the atomic-powered spaceship Explorer I has been carrying you towards the giant planet Jupiter, at 160,000 kilometres per hour. You have left on an expedition to the Unknown.

Three of your crewmates are sleeping a dreamless sleep of artificial hibernation. Since the voyage began, they have been lying in individual hibernacula, their pulse and breathing close to zero. They will be awakened only when their expertise is required – very soon now.

For the vast sphere of Jupiter is hazily visible now in front of you.

Obviously there cannot be any life of any kind here in this glacial cold, so far from the sun! But you follow a precise route that leads you across the solar system; you believe there is 'something' here, even though you cannot imagine what it is. It could be good or bad, or completely indifferent – but you must know.

And It has been awaiting your arrival for millions of years.

Glossary

This brief glossary explains certain specific terms employed in this book, and which belong to the vocabulary I have created for audiovisual analysis. Most of the definitions are taken from my book *Audio-vision: Sound on Screen*.

Acousmatic: Pertaining to sound one hears without seeing its source. Radio and telephones are acousmatic media. In a film an off-screen sound is acousmatic.

Acousmêtre: from **acousmatic** and **être** (being): a kind of voice-character specific to cinema that in most instances of cinematic narratives derives mysterious powers from being heard and not seen. See *acousmêtres* in *The Invisible Man, Das Testament des Dr Mabuse, The Wizard of Oz.*

Added value: The expressive and/or informative value with which a sound enriches a given image, so as to create the definitive impression (either immediate or remembered) that this meaning emanates 'naturally' from the image itself.

Materialising sound indices: Sonic details that supply information about the concrete materiality of sound production in the film space – for example, a pianist's breathing and fingernails on the piano keys. Sparse materialising sound indices give the impression of perfection, ethereality, abstraction.

Objective-internal sound: Designates a sound heard from inside by one character and that character alone: the sound of breathing, certain physiological sounds or creaking of bones, of the head, certain tones or hisses in the ear; but physically existing and not coming from the character's imagination.

'On the air': Sound heard in a film narrative that is supposedly transmitted by radio, video or another electronic signal and that consequently is not subject to 'natural' laws of sound propagation.

Verbo-decentred: as opposed to the heavily dominant **verbocentric** cinema, verbo-decentred cinema is that in which speech is not the implicit or explicit centre of the *mise en scène* or the narrative, even though it may still have an important role.

Credits

Original title: 2001: A SPACE ODYSSEY
Director: Stanley Kubrick
Screenplay: Stanley Kubrick and Arthur C. Clarke, based on Arthur C. Clarke's short story 'The Sentinel'
Producer: Stanley Kubrick (officially: 'Metro-Goldwyn-Mayer presents a Stanley Kubrick Production')
Assistant producer: Victor Lyndon
Assistant to the producer: Roger Caras
Second assistant producer: Ivor Powell
First assistant director: Derek Cracknell
Assistant director: Jonathan Mills
Director of photography: Goeffrey Unsworth, B.S.C.
Additional photography: John Alcott
Camera operator: Kevin Pike
Assistant camera operator: Peter MacDonald
Special photographic effects: Designed and directed by Stanley Kubrick
Special photographic effects supervisors: Wally Veevers, Douglas Trumbull, Con Pederson, Tom Howard
Special photographic effects unit: Colin J. Cantwell, Bruck Logan, Bryan Loftus, Frederick Martin, David Osborne, John Jack Malick
Art director: John Hoesli
Production designers: Tony Masters, Harry Lange, Ernie Archer
Set designer: John Graysmark
Sets: Robert Cartwright
Costumes: Hardy Amies
Make-up: Stuart Freeborn
Creator of the Star-Child sculpture: Liz Moore
Film editor: Ray Lovejoy, assisted by David de Wilde
Sound editor: Winston Ryder
Sound supervisor: A.W. Watkins

Sound mixer: H. L. Bird
Chief dubbing mixer: J. B. Smith
Scientific consultant: Frederick I. Ordway III
Music: Richard Strauss, *Also Sprach Zarathustra*;[1] Johann Strauss Jr., *Am schönen blauen Donau* (The 'Blue Danube') performed by the Berlin Philharmonic Orchestra conducted by Herbert von Karajan; Aram Khachaturian, Adagio from the ballet *Gayaneh* performed by the Leningrad Philharmonic Orchestra conducted by Gennadi Rozhdestvensky; Gyorgy Ligeti, *Atmosphères*, performed by the Southwest German Radio Orchestra conducted by Ernest Bour; Ligeti, *Lux aeterna*, performed by the Stuttgart Schola Cantorum conducted by Clytus Gottwald; Ligeti, *Requiem*, performed by the Bavarian Radio Orchestra conducted by Francis Travis.

Filmed in Super Panavision
Technicolor, Metrocolor
Made at MGM British Studios Ltd, Borehamwood, England; in Cinerama
Running time: 160 minutes (original length), shortened to 141 minutes in the official cut by Kubrick
American release: April 1968

Cast: Keir Dullea (David Bowman), Gary Lockwood (Frank Poole), William Sylvester (Dr Heywood Floyd), Douglas Rain (voice of Hal), Daniel Richter (Moonwatcher), Leonard Rossiter (Smyslov), Margaret Tyzack (Elena), Robert Beatty (Halvorsen), Sean Sullivan (Michaels), Frank Miller (Mission Controller), Alan Gifford (Poole's father), Penny Brahms (Orion stewardess), Edwina Carroll (Aries stewardess), Vivian Kubrick (Floyd's daughter), Burnell Tucker (photographer), Glenn Beck, Bill Weston, Mike Lovell, Edward Bishop, Ann Gillis, Heather Downham, John Ashley, Jimmy Bell, David Charkham, Simon Davis, Jonathan Daw, Peter Delmar, Terry Duggan, David Fleetwood, Danny Grover, Brian Hawley, David Hines, Tony Jackson, John Jordan, Scott Mackee, Laurence Marchant, Darryl Paes, Joe Refalo, Andy Wallace, Bob Wilyman, Richard Wood.

Note

1 For some reason, the official credits do not specify who performed this excerpt. Recordings of the 'original score' of the film reproduce the version by the Berlin Philharmonic conducted by Karl Böhm, indicated in most of the filmographies as the version used in the film.

Selected Bibliography

Dialogue and Shot Breakdown
'2001: Odyssée de l'espace', L'Avant-Scène, nos. 231/2, 1979. Special double science-fiction issue, with *The Invasion of the Body Snatchers* by Don Siegel. Essay on *2001* by Jacques Goimard. Shot breakdown by Dominique Abonyl. Documentation including publicity excerpts; illustrations.

On the Film
Agel, Jerome, *The Making of Kubrick's 2001* (New York and London: New American Library and Hutchinson, 1968); paperback edition, April 1970, the Agel Publishing Company, Signet. *Contains, among other texts, a long interview with Kubrick, witness accounts, a detailed press selection, a 96-page illustrated section on the shooting of the film and the production of its special effects, a series of letters from viewers, the text of Clarke's short story 'The Sentinel'. Presented with humour – not always carefully documented.*

Bizony, Piers, *2001: Filming the Future* (London: Aurum Press, 1994). *With a foreword by Arthur C. Clarke. History of the film, with very interesting illustrations that do not overlap with Agel.*

Clarke, Arthur C., *The Lost Worlds of 2001* (New York: New American Library, Signet, 1972). *The genesis of the film, narrated by the co-author of the screenplay.*

Dumont, Jean-Paul and Monod, Jean, *Le Foetus astral* (Paris: Éditions Christian Bourgeois, 1970). *Fascinating Lévi-Straussian structural analysis.*

Geduld, Carolyn, *Filmguide to 2001: A Space Odyssey* (Bloomington: Indiana University Press, 1973).

Schwam, Stephanie (ed.), *The Making of 2001: A Space Odyssey* (New York: Modern Library, 2000). Introduction by Jay Cocks, Series Editor

Martin Scorsese. *Reprints much of Agel, plus fine new essays by Simson Garfinkel, Alexander Walker, Piers Bizony*.

Stork, David G. (ed.), *Hal's Legacy* (Cambridge, Mass., MIT Press, 1997). *Articles by various writers, regarding what has become feasible and what remains remote in the 'possibilities' of the computer in Kubrick's film: recognition of visual and auditory forms, the possibility of conversing, the question of malfunctioning, consciousness.*

The Short Story and Novels of the 2001 Saga

Clarke, Arthur C., 'The Sentinel', *short story reprinted most recently in the work edited by Schwam (see above).*

Clarke, Arthur C., *2001: A Space Odyssey* (New York: Signet, New American Library, 1968), *based on a screenplay by Stanley Kubrick and Arthur C. Clarke.*

Clarke, Arthur C., *2010: Odyssey Two* (New York: Mass Market Paperback [reissue], 1984).

Clarke, Arthur C., *2061: Odyssey Three* (New York: Mass Market Paperback [reissue], 1991).

Clarke, Arthur C., *3001: The Final Odyssey* (New York: Mass Market Paperback [reissue], 1998).

On Kubrick

Bouineau, Jean-Marc, *Le Petit livre de Stanley Kubrick* (Garches: Spartorange, 1991).

Chion, Michel, *La Voix au cinéma* (Paris: Cahiers du cinéma/Éditions de l'Étoile, 1982), pp. 49–51 (*The Voice in Cinema*, trans. Claudia Gorbman [New York: Columbia University Press, 1999], pp. 44–6.

Chion, Michel, *La Musique au cinéma* (Paris: Fayard, 1995), pp. 345–52.

Ciment, Gilles (ed.), *Stanley Kubrick* (Paris: Dossiers Positif/Rivages, 1987). *Collection of articles and interviews.*

Ciment, Michel, *Kubrick* (Paris: Calmann-Lévy, rev. edn, 1987). *A detailed study, followed by Ciment's interviews with Kubrick and other collaborators; numerous illustrations.*

Falsetto, Mario, *Stanley Kubrick: A Narrative and Stylistic Analysis* (London and Westport, Conn.: Praeger, 1994). *Dense study, based on close analysis.*

Falsetto, Mario (ed.), *Perspectives on Stanley Kubrick* (New York: G. K. Hall, 1996). *Various interviews of Kubrick, and essays on the films, including Herb Lightman, Douglas Trumbull and David G. Hoch on* 2001.

Ghezzi, Enrico, *Stanley Kubrick* (Milan: L'Unità/Il Castoro cinema, 1995).

Giuliani, Pierre, *Stanley Kubrick* (Paris: Rivages, 1990).

Kagan, Norman, *Le Cinéma de Stanley Kubrick* (Paris: L'Age de l'homme, 1987).

LoBrutto, Vincent, *Stanley Kubrick: A Biography* (New York: Donald I. Fine Books, 1997).

Articles on Kubrick and *2001*

Birkin, Andrew, 'Stanley Kubrick au travail', interview by Christophe d'Yvoire, *Studio*, no. 144, April 1999, pp. 118–19. *Birkin served as assistant on* 2001.

Ciment, Michel, 'L'Odyssée de Stanley Kubrick', *Positif*, no. 98, October 1968.

Elsholz, J ean-Marc, '*2001: L'Odyssée de l'espace*, Le grand oeuvre', *Positif*, no. 439, September 1997. *Alchemical and numerological reading of the film*.

Goimard, Jacques, 'Une Odyssée formelle', *L'Avant-scène*, nos. 231/2, 1979. *Includes excellent description of the making of the film*.

Gras, Claude-Alexis, 'La Quadrature du cercle', *Tausend Augen*, no. 10, August 1997. *Kandinskyan reading, based on formal symbolism*.

Hoët, Sébastien, 'La Pierre d'absence', *Tausend Augen*, no. 10, August 1997.

Sineux, Michel, 'Maestro, musique! Image et son dans le cinéma de Stanley Kubrick', *Positif*, no. 186, October 1974.

Townson, Robert, 'The Odyssey of Alex North's *2001*', liner notes for the CD of Alex North's music (Varese I–AB 19–87).

On Science-fiction Cinema

Bouyxou, Jean-Pierre, *La Science-fiction au cinéma* (Paris: Union Générale d'Éditions, collection 10/18, 1971).

Schlockoff, Alain (ed.), 'Demain la science-fiction' (Paris: Cinéma d'aujourd'hui, no. 7, 1976).